Wheat-Free, Gluten-Free
Cookbook for Kids
and Busy Adults

Wheat-Free, Gluten-Free
Cookbook for Kids
and Busy Adults

Connie Sarros

Contemporary Books

Chicago   New York   San Francisco   Lisbon   London   Madrid   Mexico City
Milan   New Delhi   San Juan   Seoul   Singapore   Sydney   Toronto

Library of Congress Cataloging-in-Publication Data

Sarros, Connie.
    Wheat-free, gluten-free cookbook for kids and busy adults / Connie Sarros—1st ed.
      p.   cm.
    ISBN 0-07-142374-5
    1. Wheat-free diet—Recipes.   2. Gluten-free diet—Recipes.   3. Children—Nutrition.
    4. Quick and easy cookery.   I. Title.

    RM237.87.S268   2003
    641.5'63—dc21   2003012697

1 2 3 4 5 6 7 8 9 0   AGM/AGM   2 1 0 9 8 7 6 5 4 3

ISBN 0-07-142374-5

Interior design by Sue Hartman
Interior illustrations by Jacqueline Dubé and Dean Stanton, Birch Design Studios

McGraw-Hill books are available at special quantity discounts to use as premiums and sales promotions, or for use in corporate training programs. For more information, please write to the Director of Special Sales, Professional Publishing, McGraw-Hill, Two Penn Plaza, New York, NY 10121-2298. Or contact your local bookstore.

This book is printed on acid-free paper.

I dedicate this book to four very important groups of people.

*First, to all the young children with celiac disease.
You deserve to have fun in the kitchen,
making foods that are easy to prepare and good to eat.*

*Second, to busy adults who want to provide nourishing meals
but don't have a lot of time to spend in the kitchen.*

*Third, to Diane Eve Paley,
president of Celiac Sprue Association/USA, Inc.,
who inspired me to write this book.*

*Last, but certainly not least, I dedicate this book to
my wonderful children, who urged me to pursue this venture.
My daughter, Sherri, was my chief proofreader and editor.
My son, Phil, and daughter-in-law, Stacey, helped me
by giving me the valuable commodity of time.
They would bring dinner over when I was busy
all day at the computer, typing the recipes.
Their love and support helped make this book a reality.*

Contents

Preface

Eating gluten-free means you may eat almost everything—you just have to learn to prepare it with "safe" ingredients. Never use anything that contains wheat, malt, barley, or rye; most persons with celiac disease stay away from oats because of cross-contamination. Younger cooks unsure whether ingredients are safe should ask an adult before using them. There will be occasions when people will serve gluten products, such as when the baseball team orders pizza or you go to a dinner party. If you know about these events in advance, prepare for them by taking your own gluten-free pizza or checking with the host or hostess to determine whether you should bring your own food. If you are invited to a wedding reception, have an adult call the hotel or caterer to explain your diet restrictions and have a special meal prepared for you.

Ask an adult in your home if you may help with the meal planning. Start off small by planning a side dish, then making it yourself. Gradually build up to planning and cooking an entire meal. When planning your meal, think about the foods your family likes to eat. Think about color on the plate; meals look much more appetizing when they have a variety of colors and textures. You wouldn't want to serve three white foods.

Vegetables provide your body with the vitamins and nutrients it needs to grow strong, so include them with every meal. There is a saying "You are what you eat." What you eat will contribute to how you feel and how you look.

Many of the recipes in this book tell how to adjust the recipe for diabetics and milk-free diets. If you have diabetes, adjusting the recipe does not mean you may eat all you want of it. Have an adult keep a record of the sugar and carbohydrate counts you eat each day.

None of the recipes in this book require the use of a mixer; but some do call for a blender. Always have an adult present when using any electrical appliance, including a blender, the stove, or a microwave oven. Before using any knives to cut meats, vegetables, or fruits, ask for adult supervision. Onions especially may be very slippery to cut. Always take care to keep fingers away from the knife's sharp edge.

Children differ in age and ability. Adults differ in desire, aptitude, and time available for culinary creations. The recipes in this book offer something for every age group. There are simple recipes requiring only three ingredients, a bowl, and a spoon. Others are more complicated. Look over the ingredients and the equipment needed to select the dishes you feel comfortable making.

Hints for Successful Gluten-Free Cooking

Cooking without wheat or gluten is not hard. But like any skill, success in the kitchen takes practice. You can cook successfully—and safely—by practicing and by following the hints given here. This section includes ideas for alternatives to wheat flour. Lists in this section tell you how to get organized and work safely. You'll also find suggestions for planning tasty and nutritious snacks and meals.

Gluten-Free Flour Mixtures

Baking can be so much fun when you experiment with different flour mixtures. Have an adult help you pick out "safe" flours. Here are some examples:

Rice flour
Corn flour
Potato flour

Tapioca flour
Sweet rice flour
Potato starch flour
Sorghum flour
Teff flour
Fava bean flour
Buckwheat flour
Mung bean flour
Garbanzo bean flour

There are *so* many choices and *so* many possible combinations. Just be sure that you don't use any wheat flour, rye, barley, or malt—these will do damage to your insides.

By combining the flours in different amounts, you will get different results. The following recipe is for a mixture that will work well when you are making muffins, cookies, cakes, pie crusts, doughnuts, quick breads—almost anything you want to bake.

Gluten-Free Flour Mixture

2½ cups rice flour
1 cup potato starch flour
1 cup tapioca flour
¼ cup cornstarch
¼ cup bean flour
2 tablespoons xanthan gum

1. Sift the rice flour, potato starch flour, tapioca flour, cornstarch, bean flour, and xanthan gum together in a large mixing bowl.
2. Store the flour mixture in a reclosable plastic bag. Refrigerate it until you are ready to bake. If you won't be baking for a week or so, store it in the freezer. You don't have to thaw the flour mixture before using it. Just measure the amount you

will need for your recipe, and leave it at room temperature for 15 minutes before using it.

Makes 5 cups

If you are allergic to corn, omit the cornstarch from the flour mixture.

Xanthan gum, despite its intimidating name, is a simple white powder sold in pouches or small jars at health food stores.

Kitchen Hints

The following hints tell how to be organized and safe in the kitchen:

- Ask an adult for permission before cooking any recipe.
- Read the whole recipe before you begin cooking. Make sure you have all the ingredients and utensils needed, and make sure you understand the directions.
- If you cannot have milk products, substitute gluten-free, milk-free margarine when the recipe calls for butter or margarine. In place of whole milk, use soy milk (unless you are allergic to soy).
- If you need to watch your fat intake, substitute skim milk for whole milk. When a recipe calls for butter or margarine, use gluten-free, low-fat margarine.
- If you need to watch your sugar, in many recipes you may use brown sugar substitute for the sugar listed in the recipe.
- Before you start mixing the ingredients, be sure you have enough time to make the recipe. Some recipes cook in an electric slow cooker for as much as 8 hours, which means you have to assemble your dinner in the morning. Others must be refrigerated for several hours before serving.

- Wash your hands with antibacterial soap before you begin cooking, when you are finished cooking, and immediately after handling fresh meat, poultry, or fish.
- Get out all the equipment and ingredients before you start to cook.
- Use metal or aluminum pans when baking cookies. The dark-coated pans will cause your cookies to burn on the bottom.
- Use only pans that are the size called for in the recipe. Using the right pan size ensures that your foods will bake evenly.
- Measure all the ingredients before you begin mixing them.
- Wash all fresh fruits, vegetables, meats, and fish in cold water before preparing the recipe.
- Be very careful when opening cans. The cut edges on the can and on the lid are very sharp.
- Ask an adult to help you whenever a recipe calls for boiling water or using a microwave, stove, oven, sharp knife, scissors, grater, peeler, or any electrical appliance.
- Whenever you use a blender, be sure an adult is present. Always put the cover or lid on a blender before turning it on.
- When cooking on the stove, turn all pot handles away from you so the pots won't be knocked over accidentally.
- If you are making a sticky or fluffy batter, wet your spatula or hands before patting or spreading the batter in the pan.
- Use thick, dry pot holders to handle all hot pots, pans, casseroles, and baking sheets.
- Clean the countertops and utensils as you use them.
- Wipe floor spills as soon as they happen. Keeping floors clean prevents you and others in the kitchen from slipping.
- Don't lift the lid from a slow cooker while cooking, especially during the first three-fourths of the cooking time.

The heat lost during a quick peek will add 30 minutes to the cooking time.

- When you cook in an electric slow cooker, vegetables take longer to cook than meat does. For that reason, place vegetables on the bottom of the pot.
- After you serve your food, your pan may be crusted and difficult to clean. Put a few drops of dish soap in the pan, and add warm water. Then let the pan soak awhile. The stuck-on food should clean off easily after soaking.
- If you get fruit stains on your fingers, you can remove the stains by rubbing your hands with vinegar.
- Many of the recipes in this book have diabetic and milk-free adjustments. If you have diabetes, this does not mean that you may eat all you want of these recipes. Have an adult keep record of the sugar and carbohydrate counts you eat each day.

Including Vegetables When Planning Meals

Planning a meal is as creative as painting a picture. Think about colors, textures, and good nutrition. Every meal should include vegetables. They may be in different forms:

- A salad
- A cooked side dish
- Part of a stew or casserole (mixed in with the meat and starch)

If you want a simple vegetable, steam one of the vegetables in the following list (fresh, frozen, or canned). Put about ½ inch of water in a saucepan and add the vegetable. Bring the water to a boil, and simmer the vegetables a few minutes until tender-crisp. Have an adult help you remove the hot pan from the stove and drain the vegetables in a strainer. Add a little butter, gluten-free margarine, or oil and a dash of salt and pepper. You have just made a delicious vegetable side dish. The following vegetables can be steamed:

Asparagus
Broccoli
Brussels sprouts
Butter beans
Cabbage
Carrots
Corn
Green beans
Italian green beans
Lima beans
Mushrooms
Peas
Potatoes (white, sweet, or
    yams)
Snow peas
Spinach
Zucchini

Another way to get creative is to make a beautiful salad. When making a salad, you may use one kind of lettuce or a variety of greens. Here are some of the possibilities:

Bibb lettuce
Dandelion greens
Endive
Iceberg lettuce
Leaf lettuce
Radicchio

Red leaf lettuce
Romaine lettuce
Spinach
Watercress

Along with greens, it's fun to add beans and other vegetables. Try some of these:

Beets
Bell peppers
Black beans
Black olives
Broccoli
Carrots
Cauliflower
Celery
Corn
Cucumbers
Garbanzo beans
Green beans
Green olives
Kidney beans
Mushrooms
Onion slices
Peas
Pepperoncini
Radishes
Tomatoes
Zucchini

Cooking with Few Ingredients

Are you looking for something that uses just a few ingredients? The following recipes use five or fewer ingredients:

Apple and Pear Dip
Apple-Cranberry Punch
Apricotberry Drink
Baked Ham Slices
Boston Cooler
Chocolate Banana Drink
Chocolate Candy
Chocolate Popcorn
Chocolate Soda
Cinnamon Baked Apples
Cinnamon Hot Chocolate
Corned Beef and Cabbage
Cranberry Mold
Crunchy Ice-Cream Sandwiches
Crunchy Pumpkin Seeds
Dilled Peas
Dipping Sauce for Fruit
Flower Pot Sundaes
Frozen Banana Sticks
Fruity Pops
Ham and Egg Cups
Homemade Peanut Butter
Hot Banana Sundae
Ice-Cream Sandwich
Lime Fizz
Lunch Meat Rolls
Mashed Breakfast
Mint Lemon Fizz
No-Bake Peanut Butter Cookies
No-Cook Applesauce
Orange Beets
Paintbrush Cookies
Peach Slush

Peanut Butter Baked Apples
Peanut Butter Candy
Peanut Butter Cookies
Peanut Butter Logs
Peanut Butter Pops
Peanut Butter Smoothie
Pepperoni Bites
Pineapple Berry Cooler
Pineberry Drink
Potato Buffet
Purple Pops
Raspberry Cooler
Raspberry Whip
Slow-Cooker Hot Dogs
Slow-Cooker Pork Chops
Slow-Cooker Sausage
Snack-Ems
Snowman Treat
Spicy Cheese Spread
Super-Easy Chicken
Tortilla Snack

Cooking at the Last Minute

You have soccer practice (or bagpipe lessons, or whatever) after school. By the time you get home, you are starving. You want a meal that will take only a few minutes to prepare and not much time to cook. No problem. The following dishes will be table-ready in 35 minutes or less:

Almost Cheeseburger
Cheesy Tomatoes
Dilled Peas
Glazed Yams

Hot Dog Burrito
Italian Marinated Salad
Lunch Meat Rolls
Mexican Rice
No-Cook Applesauce
Orange Beets
Parmesan Fish
Polka-Dot Rice
Potato and Broccoli Casserole
Seasoned French Fries
Skillet Supper
Spinach and Rice
Spinach with Cheese
Strawberry Spinach Salad
Super-Easy Chicken
Taco Casserole
Tortilla Tower
Tuna Melt

Cooking Ahead

Sometimes you want to cook, but you won't be home in time to prepare dinner. Fortunately, a lot of meals may be assembled in advance, covered and refrigerated, then baked just before you are ready to eat. Here are some recipes that can be cooked ahead of time:

All-in-One Dinner
Baked Ham Slices
Breaded Veggies
Buffalo Wings
Cheesy Chicken

Chicken Kabobs
Corn Casserole
Creamy Potatoes
Glazed Yams
Meat Loaf Muffins
Night-Before Oven French Toast
Night-Before Breakfast Casserole
Oven-Fried Chicken
Potato and Broccoli Casserole
Spaghetti Pie

Slow cookers are great when you will be gone all day. You combine everything in the morning, put it in the pot, turn it on low, put the lid on the pot, then go to school, to the beach in the summer, or wherever. When you return home at the end of your busy day, your dinner is ready! Here are some great slow-cooker casseroles:

Corned Beef and Cabbage
Country Ribs
Macaroni and Cheese
Mexican Toss Casserole
Slow-Cooker Hot Dogs
Slow-Cooker Pork Chops
Slow-Cooker Sausage
Slow-Cooker Steak
Super-Easy Chicken

No-Help Recipes

Do you want to surprise an adult by creating something for her or him from the kitchen? If so, you need a recipe that does not use the stove, oven, blender, or other electrical appliance. Here are some recipes that are easy to make:

Apple-Cranberry Punch
Boston Cooler
Cherry Whip Pudding
Chocolate Soda
Cole Slaw
Cranberry Punch
Crunchy Ice-Cream Sandwiches
Flower Pot Sundaes
Frozen Banana Sticks
Fruity Pops
Ice-Cream Sandwich
Italian Marinated Salad
Lime Fizz
Lunch Meat Rolls
Mashed Breakfast
Mint Lemon Fizz
Mixed Bean Salad
No-Bake Peanut Butter Cookies
Peanut Butter Logs
Pepperoni Bites
Personalized Parfaits
Pineberry Drink
Rice Cake Bonanza
Strawberry Spinach Salad
Trail Mix
Winter Fruit Bowl

Cooking Basics

Measurements

    1 tablespoon = 3 teaspoons

    1 fluid ounce = 2 tablespoons

    1 jigger = 3 tablespoons

    ¼ cup = 4 tablespoons

    ⅓ cup = 5⅓ tablespoons

    ½ cup = 8 tablespoons

    1 cup = ½ pint = 16 tablespoons

    1 cup = 8 fluid ounces

    1 pint = 2 cups

    1 quart = 4 cups = 2 pints

    ½ gallon = 2 quarts

    1 gallon — 4 quarts

    ½ stick butter = 4 tablespoons = ¼ cup

    1 stick butter = 8 tablespoons = ½ cup

    1 pound butter = 4 sticks = 2 cups

    1 pound = 16 ounces

    1 pound granulated sugar = 2¼ cups

    1 pound brown sugar = 2¼ cups, packed down

1 pound confectioners' sugar = 3½ cups
1 square baking chocolate = 1 ounce

Emergency Substitutions

If you are missing an ingredient, check this list to see if you can substitute something else:

1 square gluten-free unsweetened chocolate = 3
  tablespoons cocoa + 1 tablespoon butter (margarine
  may be used in place of butter, but it will not heat as well
  as butter does)
1 ounce gluten-free semisweet or milk chocolate = ⅓ cup
  chocolate chips
2 tablespoons Gluten-Free Flour Mixture for thickening =
  1½ tablespoons cornstarch
1 teaspoon gluten-free baking powder = ¼ teaspoon
  baking soda + ½ teaspoon cream of tartar +
  ¼ teaspoon cornstarch
1 cup corn syrup = 1 cup sugar + ¼ cup liquid (same type
  as liquid used in the recipe)
1 tablespoon cornstarch (for thickening) = 4 teaspoons
  quick-cooking tapioca
1 cup sugar = 1 cup honey or 1 cup maple syrup (reduce
  other liquid in recipe by ⅓ cup)
1 cup half-and-half = 1 cup evaporated milk = ½ cup milk
  + ½ cup cream
1 cup milk = ½ cup evaporated milk + ½ cup water
1 cup buttermilk = 1 tablespoon apple cider vinegar +
  enough milk to make 1 cup
1 cup firmly packed brown sugar = 1 cup white sugar +
  2 tablespoons molasses

1 cup firmly packed brown sugar = 1 cup brown sugar
    substitute (sold near granulated sugar in grocery stores)

1 package gluten-free active dry yeast = 1 tablespoon
    gluten-free active dry yeast

3 tablespoons cream of tartar = 2 tablespoons gluten-free
    baking powder + 1 tablespoon baking soda

1 cup ketchup = 1 cup tomato sauce + ½ cup sugar +
    2 tablespoons cider vinegar

1 cup canned tomatoes = 1⅓ cups cut-up fresh tomatoes
    simmered 10 minutes

1 tablespoon fresh herbs = 1 teaspoon dried herbs

1 clove garlic = ⅛ teaspoon garlic powder

Cooking Techniques

Baking: When baking, place food on the center rack in the oven, unless otherwise stated in the recipe. Leave at least 2 inches of space around the pan. Overcrowding causes uneven cooking.

Most baked items will cook in the amount of time indicated in each recipe. However, ovens vary. So check the baked item about 5 minutes before it should be done so it doesn't dry out or burn. You might have to leave something baking longer than indicated in the recipe. To test whether cakes, muffins, and sweet breads are done baking, insert a toothpick in the center and pull it back out. If it comes out dry, the product is done cooking.

Always remember to use pot holders when removing anything from the oven.

Bell Peppers: To clean a bell pepper, cut it in half, then in quarters. Remove all the seeds and the thick white membrane inside the shell.

Boiling Over: Before you cook rice or macaroni, butter the rim of the pan. It will keep the water from boiling over.

Cakes: To keep a cake fresh longer, place half an apple in the cake container when you store it.

Candy: Try to make your candy on dry days. Candy does not set as well on humid or rainy days.

Casseroles: Most casseroles may be made up to 24 hours in advance and refrigerated. Some refrigerated casserole containers, like Pyrex and stainless steel, may be placed in a preheated oven. Other cold pans, like glass dishes, must be placed in a cold oven before the heat is turned on. (When a cold glass dish is placed in a cold oven, the dish will warm slowly as the oven heats, preventing the glass from shattering.)

Chilling Foods: To chill foods quickly, put them in your freezer for 20 to 30 minutes, rather than longer in the refrigerator.

Chopping Onions: To prevent your eyes from watering when you chop onions, place a quarter of a slice of bread between your teeth. Allow it to stick out of your mouth a little, and keep your mouth slightly open. Now you can chop the onions, and you will have no tears or burning eyes.

Cookies: To keep cookies soft, place a slice of soft, gluten-free bread in the storage container.

To prevent cookies from spreading when baking, refrigerate the dough on the baking sheet for 30 minutes before baking.

If you want your cookies to have the same size and appearance, use a cookie scoop (or a small ice-cream scoop) to spoon out the cookie dough. This method also keeps your fingers clean.

Corn: When boiling corn on the cob, add a pinch of sugar to the water to help bring out the corn's natural sweetness.

Dash: Whenever a measurement is less than ⅛ teaspoon, the recipe will call for a "dash." To add a dash, sprinkle in just a teeny bit of the ingredient.

Eggs: A fresh egg's shell is rough and chalky looking. An old egg will have a shell that is smooth and shiny. Another way to check an egg's freshness is to place the egg in a pot of cold, salted water. If the egg sinks, it is fresh. If it floats, it is not fresh, so throw it away!

If you see any red specks in an egg, throw out the egg.

Do you have eggs in your refrigerator, and you don't know if they are raw or hard-boiled? Spin the egg. If it spins, it is hard-boiled. If it wobbles, it is raw.

It is easier to separate egg yolks from egg whites when the eggs are cold.

To prevent eggshells from cracking when you boil eggs, add a pinch of salt to the water.

Frozen Vegetables: A quick way to separate frozen vegetables for use in a casserole is to put the vegetables in a colander, set the colander in the sink, and pour boiling water over the vegetables.

Fudge: Always use a wooden spoon when making fudge.

Gelatin Molds: To easily unmold gelatin salads or desserts, lightly brush the mold with oil or spray it with gluten-free nonstick spray before pouring in the mixture.

Glass Baking Dishes: When using a glass baking dish for cakes, lower the oven temperature by 25 degrees.

Juicing Citrus Fruits: To get the most juice out of fresh lemons, limes, and oranges, bring them to room temperature, then roll them under your palm against the kitchen countertop before squeezing.

Measurements: Dry products should be measured in one of a nest of measuring cups so the top may be leveled off with a knife.

When measuring brown sugar, pack it down into the cup as tightly as possible. Never pack down flour or white sugar. Instead, lightly spoon it into the measuring cup.

Liquids should be measured in a glass measuring cup. To get the correct reading, set the cup on the counter and stoop down so the measuring line is at eye level.

Measuring Corn Syrup, Molasses, and Honey: Before you measure sticky ingredients like corn syrup, molasses, or honey, dip the measuring cup or spoon in hot water or brush it with vegetable oil. This will help prevent sticking and make it easier to pour out the measured ingredient.

Meatballs: When making many meatballs, a fast and simple way to get uniform sizes is to shape the entire meat mixture into a square, then cut it into cubes. Roll each cube into a meatball.

Onions: To clean an onion, cut a slice off each end. Peel off the outer layer to remove all the yellow (or red or white) skin.

Pancakes: Use a turkey baster to squeeze your pancake batter onto the hot griddle. You'll get perfectly shaped pancakes every time.

Pies: For a flakier crust, substitute 1 teaspoon of vinegar for 1 teaspoon of the cold water called for in the recipe.

When cutting cream pies, first dip your knife into hot water. That keeps the filling from sticking to the knife.

Potatoes: Most of the recipes in this book do not tell you to peel the potatoes. Much of the nutritional value of a potato is found in its skin. Be sure to wash the outside of the potato before cooking.

Preheating Oven: Turn on the oven about 10 minutes before you bake anything, unless you are using a glass dish. Most ovens take this long to reach the preset temperature.

Sautéing: Many recipes have you cook vegetables, meats, rice, and even nuts by sautéing them. This means putting a little bit of oil or butter in a skillet and quickly searing the ingredients over high heat, stirring frequently.

Shredding Cheese: To shred cheese easily, let the cheese sit in the freezer for 30 minutes before shredding.

Sifting Dry Ingredients: Gluten-free flours are heavier than wheat flour, so they definitely need to be sifted just before you add them to a recipe. You may sift the dry ingredients together onto a sheet of waxed paper, then curl up two opposite edges to transfer the flours to a bowl. Or you may sift the flour mixture directly over the bowl containing the other ingredients.

The easiest way to sift is to use a sieve large enough to hold all of the ingredients to be sifted. With the edge of a spoon, scrape along the inside of the sieve, forcing the flours through the tiny holes.

Soups: To remove some of the fat in soups, add a lettuce leaf to the pot. Remove the leaf before serving. If your soup is too salty, add a raw potato that has been cut in half. The potato will absorb some of the salt. Remove the potato before serving.

Temperature for Baking: Do not increase the oven temperature above that recommended in the recipe. It won't speed up the cooking process. Your product will burn on the outside, and it will not be cooked on the inside.

Wooden Skewers: When using wooden skewers for kabobs, soak them in cold water for 30 minutes before stringing foods. Soaking prevents skewers from burning during cooking.

1

Snacks

Cereal Candy

3 cups gluten-free puffed-rice cereal

⅓ cup raisins

⅓ cup dried cranberries

⅓ cup peanuts

6 ounces chocolate chips

2 tablespoons light corn syrup

1 Mix the cereal, raisins, cranberries, and peanuts on a cookie sheet.

2 Have an adult help you melt the chocolate chips in a double boiler over steaming water or in the microwave. When the chocolate has melted, stir in the corn syrup.

3 Carefully drizzle the melted chocolate evenly over the cereal mix. Stir to mix.

4 Spoon into cupcake papers.

5 Set cupcake papers on a clean cookie sheet. Place in the refrigerator for 30 minutes to set the chocolate.

Makes 9 ½-cup servings

One serving—Calories: 230; Total fat: 8.4 g; Saturated fat: 4.6 g; Cholesterol: 0 mg; Sodium: 154 mg; Carbohydrates: 38 g; Fiber: 1.8 g; Sugar: 25.3 g; Protein: 3 g

Peanut Butter Candy

2 cups nonfat dry milk

1 cup honey

1 cup gluten-free peanut butter

1 cup semisweet chocolate chips

1. In a large bowl, stir together the milk and honey. Let the mixture set for 20 minutes.
2. With your hands, mix in the peanut butter. Knead the mixture until smooth. Roll into bite-sized balls, and place them on an ungreased baking sheet. Refrigerate the balls for 1 hour or until firm.
3. Have an adult help you melt the chocolate in a double boiler over barely simmering water, or melt it in the microwave. When the chocolate has melted, dip half of each ball into the chocolate, then put it back on the baking sheet. Refrigerate the candy until the chocolate has set, about ½ hour.

Makes 16 ¼-cup servings

One serving—Calories: 593; Total fat: 40 g; Saturated fat: 9 g; Cholesterol: 16 mg; Sodium: 300 mg; Carbohydrates: 42.4 g; Fiber: 4.7 g; Sugar: 27 g; Protein: 23 g

Caramel Popcorn

¼ cup gluten-free margarine

½ cup brown sugar

2 tablespoons corn syrup

2 tablespoons honey

¼ teaspoon baking soda

4 cups popped popcorn

1 cup broken walnuts

1. Put the margarine, brown sugar, corn syrup, and honey in a large microwave-safe bowl. Microwave on High for 3 minutes, then stir.
2. Add the baking soda. Stir carefully until the mixture is foamy.
3. Microwave the brown sugar sauce on High for another 1½ minutes.
4. Add the popcorn and walnuts. Stir until evenly coated with brown sugar sauce.
5. Microwave the popcorn mixture for 1 minute.
6. Spread the mixture onto a large sheet of waxed paper. Let it cool at room temperature for 1 hour to set.
7. Break the mixture into pieces. Store in a gallon-size, reclosable plastic bag.

Makes 11 ½-cup servings

One serving—Calories: 134; Total fat: 8.7 g; Saturated fat: 1.3 g; Cholesterol: 0 mg; Sodium: 72 mg; Carbohydrates: 14.6 g; Fiber: 0.7 g; Sugar: 11.3 g; Protein: 1.5 g

Diabetic Adjustment: Use gluten-free, low-fat margarine in place of the regular margarine. Use brown-sugar substitute in place of the brown sugar. Omit the walnuts.

One serving—Calories: 62.5; Total fat: 3.9 g; Saturated fat: 0.9 g; Cholesterol: 0 mg; Sodium: 71 mg; Carbohydrates: 7.7 g; Fiber: 0.3 g; Sugar: 5.8 g; Protein: 0.3 g

Milk-Free Adjustment: Use gluten-free, milk-free margarine.

Trail Mix

½ cup sunflower seeds
½ cup raisins
½ cup grated, unsweetened coconut
½ cup dry-roasted peanuts
½ cup semisweet chocolate chips
½ cup dried cranberries

1. Put the sunflower seeds, raisins, coconut, peanuts, chocolate chips, and dried cranberries into a large bowl. Stir till evenly mixed.
2. Store the mix in a quart-size, reclosable plastic bag.

The beauty of Trail Mix is that you may customize it to your tastes. Each time you make it, try combining different ingredients such as cut-up dates, cut-up dried apricots, dried banana slices, walnut pieces, or gluten-free butterscotch chips in addition to or in place of the original ingredients.

Makes 12 ¼-cup servings

One serving—Calories: 134; Total fat: 6.5 g; Saturated fat: 1.9 g; Cholesterol: 0 mg; Sodium: 23 mg; Carbohydrates: 18.3 g; Fiber: 1.5 g; Sugar: 14.5 g; Protein: 1.4 g

Snack-Ems

1 stick gluten-free margarine
1 cup gluten-free peanut butter
1 12-ounce package semisweet chocolate chips
1 1-pound box gluten-free puffed-corn cereal
1 1-pound box confectioners' sugar

1. Place the margarine, peanut butter, and chocolate chips in a small microwavable bowl. Microwave on Medium (50 percent power) for 1 minute.
2. Remove the bowl from the microwave, and stir the contents.
3. Return the bowl to the microwave, and cook for 1 minute on Medium (50 percent power). Stir, and continue the process of heating and stirring until the mixture is melted.
4. Place the cereal in a large bowl. Drizzle the chocolate mixture over the top to coat the cereal evenly.
5. Stir the cereal to help distribute the chocolate coating.

6 Empty the confectioners' sugar into a paper grocery bag. Add the chocolate-coated cereal. Close the top of the bag.

7 Shake the bag until the sugar evenly coats the cereal mixture.

Makes 24 ½-cup servings

One serving—Calories: 282; Total fat: 18.8 g; Saturated fat: 5 g; Cholesterol: 4 mg; Sodium: 215 mg; Carbohydrates: 23.5 g; Fiber: 1.6 g; Sugar: 11.7 g; Protein: 6.6 g

Milk-Free Adjustment: Use gluten-free, milk-free margarine. Use gluten-free, milk-free cereal.

Rice Cake Bonanza

1 gluten-free rice cake

1 teaspoon gluten-free peanut butter

1 teaspoon gluten-free jelly (your favorite flavor)

2 teaspoons raisins

½ banana

2 teaspoons gluten-free miniature marshmallows

1 Spread the peanut butter on one side of the rice cake.

2 Spread the jelly on top of the peanut butter.

3 Sprinkle the raisins on top of the jelly.

4 Slice the banana over the raisins, then sprinkle with the marshmallows.

Makes 1 serving

One serving—Calories: 311; Total fat: 5.5 g; Saturated fat: 0.6 g; Cholesterol: 0 mg; Sodium: 49 mg; Carbohydrates: 47 g; Fiber: 3 g; Sugar: 31.5 g; Protein: 4 g

Cranberry Candy

1 15-ounce can cranberry sauce

1 cup plus 3 tablespoons granulated sugar

1 3-ounce box gluten-free raspberry gelatin

1 3-ounce box gluten-free lemon gelatin

½ cup finely chopped almonds

3 tablespoons confectioners' sugar

¼ teaspoon cinnamon

1. In a medium saucepan, stir together the cranberry sauce, 1 cup of sugar, and the raspberry and lemon gelatins.

2. Have an adult help you bring the mixture to a boil over medium heat, stirring frequently. Remove the pan from the heat, and stir in the nuts.

3. Pour the mixture into a 9-inch square pan. Let mixture cool, then put it in the refrigerator for at least 6 hours.

4. Cut the gelled mixture into 1-inch, bite-size squares.

5. Sift 3 tablespoons of granulated sugar, the confectioners' sugar, and the cinnamon together onto a piece of waxed paper. Holding both sides of the waxed paper, pour the sugar mixture into a sandwich-size, reclosable plastic bag.

6. Place four squares of gelatin into the bag. Seal the bag, and shake to coat all sides with sugar. Remove the squares, and arrange them on a plate. Repeat with the remaining squares, working in small batches.

7. When all the squares are coated with the sugar mixture, return the squares to the plastic bag. Seal it securely until ready to serve.

Makes 81 1-piece servings

One serving—Calories: 24; Total fat: 0.2 g; Saturated fat: 0 g; Cholesterol: 0 mg; Sodium: 5 mg; Carbohydrates: 6 g; Fiber: 0.1 g; Sugar: 5 g; Protein: 0.3 g

Almond Fudge

2¼ cups sugar

2 tablespoons unsweetened cocoa (*not* hot chocolate mix)

¼ cup butter

¾ cup evaporated milk

5 ounces (a little over 1 cup) gluten-free marshmallow creme

2 teaspoons almond extract

6 ounces semisweet chocolate chips

¾ cup chopped almonds

1. Put the sugar, cocoa, butter, evaporated milk, and marshmallow creme in a medium saucepan.
2. Cook on medium-high heat, stirring very frequently, until mixture comes to a full boil.
3. Lower the heat to medium and cook, stirring constantly, for 5 minutes.
4. With the help of an adult, remove the hot pan from the stove and place it on a trivet or pot holder. Stir in the almond extract and the chocolate chips until the chocolate has melted and is blended in.
5. Stir in the almonds.
6. Spray a 9-inch square pan with gluten-free nonstick spray. Spoon the mixture into the pan. Smooth the top.
7. Refrigerate the fudge for several hours until firm. Cut into 1½ inch squares to serve.

Makes 36 1-piece servings

One serving—Calories: 93; Total fat: 4.4 g; Saturated fat: 1.1 g; Cholesterol: 5 mg; Sodium: 22 mg; Carbohydrates: 12.7 g; Fiber: 0.3 g; Sugar: 11.4 g; Protein: 1 g

Chocolate Popcorn

1 cup (8 ounces) semisweet chocolate chips

1 cup freshly popped popcorn

1 cup salted peanuts

1. With an adult's help, melt chocolate chips in the top part of a double boiler over barely simmering water. (If the water is too hot, the chocolate will burn.) Or, melt in the microwave.

2) Remove pan from the stove and add the popcorn and nuts. Stir until they are evenly coated with chocolate.

3) Drop large spoonfuls of the mixture onto a cookie sheet. Let cool until firm.

Makes 12 ¼-cup servings

One serving—Calories: 17; Total fat: 6 g; Saturated fat: 3 g; Cholesterol: 0 mg; Sodium: 40 mg; Carbohydrates: 13 g; Fiber: 0.2 g; Sugar: 9.6 g; Protein: 0.8 g

Chocolate Candy

½ pound gluten-free chocolate (your choice of milk, semisweet, or white chocolate)

½ cup raisins

½ cup plain salted peanuts or cashews

1) Put the chocolate in a 2-quart glass bowl.

2) Microwave on High for about 1½ minutes (see note below).

3) Remove the bowl from the microwave. Stir the chocolate.

4) If the chocolate has not melted, return the bowl to the microwave, and continue to cook on High until shiny. Note: Semisweet chocolate will need to be heated for a total of 2 to 2½ minutes; milk chocolate needs 1½ to 1¾ minutes, and white chocolate needs 1 to 1½ minutes.

5) Remove the bowl from the microwave, and stir the chocolate until smooth.

6) Stir in the raisins and nuts.

7) Drop by teaspoonfuls onto a cookie sheet. Refrigerate until firm.

If you like, you can stir in gluten-free miniature marshmallows when you add the nuts and raisins.

Makes 20 pieces

One piece—Calories: 77; Total fat: 3.7 g; Saturated fat: 2 g; Cholesterol: 0 mg; Sodium: 22 mg; Carbohydrates: 10.8 g; Fiber: 0.3 g; Sugar: 8.6 g; Protein: 0.5 g

Milk-Free Adjustment: Use semisweet chocolate.

Tortilla Snack

1 gluten-free corn tortilla

½ teaspoon gluten-free margarine

½ teaspoon cinnamon-sugar (or ½ teaspoon sugar + ⅛ teaspoon cinnamon)

1 Preheat oven to 350°F.

2 Spread the margarine on one side of the tortilla. Sprinkle the cinnamon-sugar on top.

3 Place tortilla in a small baking pan and bake for 4 minutes. Have an adult help you remove the hot pan from the oven.

Makes 1 serving

One serving—Calories: 158; Total fat: 9.5 g; Saturated fat: 1.5 g; Cholesterol: 0 mg; Sodium: 134 mg; Carbohydrates: 18 g; Fiber: 1 g; Sugar: 1.2 g; Protein: 2 g

Crunchy Pumpkin Seeds

2 cups pumpkin seeds fresh from a pumpkin

1¼ teaspoons salt

¼ teaspoon cinnamon

1 Preheat oven to 350°F.

2 Have an adult help carve the pumpkin. Scoop out the pulp that contains the seeds. Put the pulp in a colander. Wash the pulp and stringy matter off the seeds under cold running water. Blot the seeds dry with paper towels.

3 Spread the seeds in a single layer on a cookie sheet. Sprinkle the seeds with salt, then with cinnamon.

(4) Place the cookie sheet in the oven, and bake the seeds for 10 minutes or until dry and lightly toasted. The cooking time will depend on the amount of seeds and how dry they were when they were put in the oven.

Makes 16 2-tablespoon servings

One serving—Calories: 32; Total fat: 1 g; Saturated fat: 0.2 g; Cholesterol: 0 mg; Sodium: 186 mg; Carbohydrates: 4 g; Fiber: 3 g; Sugar: 0 g; Protein: 1 g

Spicy Cheese Spread

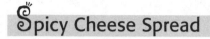

1 cup grated gluten-free sharp cheddar cheese

2 tablespoons chopped canned green chilies

¼ cup gluten-free mayonnaise

⅛ teaspoon gluten-free chili powder

2½ ounces gluten-free miniature tortilla chips

(1) Preheat broiler.

(2) In a bowl, stir together the grated cheese with the chilies, mayonnaise, and chili powder. Spread the cheese mixture over the tortilla chips.

(3) Place the chips on a cookie sheet. Broil just until cheese is slightly toasted, about 2 to 3 minutes. Have an adult help you remove the cookie sheet from the oven.

Makes 20 3-chip servings

One serving—Calories: 82; Total fat: 6 g; Saturated fat: 2 g; Cholesterol: 12 mg; Sodium: 120 mg; Carbohydrates: 3 g; Fiber: 0.2 g; Sugar: 0 g; Protein: 3 g

Taco Dip

1 16-ounce can gluten-free chili without beans

1 4½-ounce can chopped green chilies

1 tablespoon gluten-free taco seasoning mix

1 16-ounce jar gluten-free refrigerated cheese sauce or soft-
packed, refrigerated, gluten-free American cheese

90 gluten-free tortilla chips

 Put chili, green chilies, seasoning mix, and cheese sauce or cheese into a microwave-safe bowl. Heat the mixture in the microwave on High for 2 minutes. Remove the bowl, and stir contents.

2 Return the bowl to the microwave, and heat on High another 2 minutes. The bowl will be hot, so use pot holders to remove it from the microwave. Stir.

3 Serve with tortilla chips.

Makes 18 5-chip servings (¼-cup servings of dip)

One serving—Calories: 130; Total fat: 7 g; Saturated fat: 3.5 g; Cholesterol: 22 mg;
Sodium: 580 mg; Carbohydrates: 10 g; Fiber: 1 g; Sugar: 1.9 g; Protein: 7 g

Stove-Top Dip

Serve this dip with gluten-free nacho chips.

2 tablespoons olive oil

2 green onions, sliced thin

1 16-ounce can gluten-free refried beans

¼ cup water

¼ cup gluten-free salsa

¾ cup shredded gluten-free sharp cheddar cheese

1 Heat the olive oil for 20 seconds in a small saucepan.

2 Add the green onions. Sauté them lightly until they are soft.

③ Add the refried beans. Cook until the beans are soft, stirring frequently.

④ Stir in the water until blended.

⑤ Stir in the salsa until blended.

⑥ Add the cheese slowly to the mixture. Stir until the cheese is completely melted.

⑦ Remove the pan from the heat. Let the dip cool slightly before serving.

Makes 14 ¼-cup servings

One serving—Calories: 73; Total fat: 3.6 g; Saturated fat: 1.2 g; Cholesterol: 4 mg; Sodium: 210 mg; Carbohydrates: 7 g; Fiber: 1.9 g; Sugar: 0.1 g; Protein: 3.2 g

Spicy Tortilla Chips

8 gluten-free corn tortillas

2 tablespoons olive oil

2 teaspoons gluten-free
   chili powder

¾ teaspoon salt

½ teaspoon oregano

2 tablespoons chopped canned green chilies

¾ cup grated gluten-free white sharp cheddar cheese

① Preheat oven to 400°F.

② Arrange the tortillas on a large cookie sheet.

③ Brush one side of each tortilla with olive oil.

④ In a small bowl, stir the chili powder, salt, and oregano. Sprinkle the mixture over the tortillas (on the side with the olive oil).

⑤ Sprinkle the chilies on the tortillas.

⑥ Sprinkle the grated cheese on top of the chilies.

⑦ Have an adult help you use a clean pair of kitchen scissors to cut the tortillas into fourths.

⑧ Bake for 12 to 15 minutes until they are golden and crisp.

Makes 16 2-wedge servings

One serving—Calories: 108; Total fat: 7.4 g; Saturated fat: 1.8 g; Cholesterol: 5 mg; Sodium: 202 mg; Carbohydrates: 9 g; Fiber: 0.5 g; Sugar: 0 g; Protein: 2.3 g

Homemade Peanut Butter

1 cup dry-roasted, unsalted peanuts

1 tablespoon peanut oil

1 teaspoon sugar

1 Put the nuts into a blender.

2 Have an adult help you blend the nuts until they are ground fine.

3 Add the oil and blend well, stopping to scrape the sides of the blender frequently with a rubber spatula.

4 Add the sugar, and blend again until the mixture looks like peanut butter. If you like crunchy peanut butter, mix in some finely chopped peanuts.

Makes about 12 1-tablespoon servings

One serving—Calories: 78; Total fat: 7 g; Saturated fat: 0.9 g; Cholesterol: 0 mg; Sodium: 1 mg; Carbohydrates: 3.1 g; Fiber: 1 g; Sugar: 0.2 g; Protein: 2 g

Pepperoni Bites

3 ounces gluten-free cream cheese, softened

72 slices (about ½ pound) gluten-free small pepperoni slices

1 Spread a layer of cream cheese on 54 pepperoni slices.

2 Stack the pepperoni slices, cream cheese facing up, into stacks of three. Top each stack with a plain slice of pepperoni.

3 Insert a toothpick into each stack. Serve them as a snack or appetizer.

Makes 18 stacks

One stack—Calories: 71; Total fat: 7 g; Saturated fat: 3 g; Cholesterol: 13 mg; Sodium: 260 mg; Carbohydrates: 1 g; Fiber: 0 g; Sugar: 0.1 g; Protein: 3 g

Cheese Crackers

1 cup gluten-free cornflakes

1 cup grated gluten-free sharp cheddar cheese

1 teaspoon paprika

1 teaspoon oregano

½ cup Gluten-Free Flour Mixture (See the Hints chapter.)

¼ cup butter, melted

1 Preheat oven to 375°F.

2 Put the cornflakes in a plastic bag. Use a rolling pin to crush the cereal.

3 Put the cheese and cereal in a medium bowl. Add the paprika and oregano.

4 Sift the flour mixture over the cereal mixture. Stir to combine them.

5 Add the butter. With your hands, mix the ingredients until completely blended.

6 Spray a cookie sheet with gluten-free nonstick spray. Form the dough into balls, and place them on the cookie sheet.

7 Bake the cheese balls for 10 minutes.

8 Have an adult help you remove the hot cookie sheet from the oven. Leave cheese crackers on baking sheet for 3 minutes, then place in a serving dish. Serve warm.

Makes 36 crackers

One cracker—Calories: 33; Total fat: 2.4 g; Saturated fat: 0.3 g; Cholesterol: 6 mg; Sodium: 41 mg; Carbohydrates: 1.9 g; Fiber: 0 g; Sugar: 0.1 g; Protein: 1 g

2
Drinks

Lime Fizz

¼ cup cold gluten-free lemon-lime soda

¼ cup gluten-free lime sherbet

½ cup cold ginger ale

1 Pour the soda into a drinking glass.

2 Spoon the sherbet into the glass.

3 Pour in the ginger ale.

Use your imagination to combine different flavors of soda and sherbet. Try gluten-free orange sherbet with orange soda, or gluten-free lemon sherbet with cherry soda.

Makes 1 1-cup serving

One serving—Calories: 141; Total fat: 1 g; Saturated fat: 0.5 g; Cholesterol: 3 mg; Sodium: 48 mg; Carbohydrates: 33 g; Fiber: 0 g; Sugar: 31 g; Protein: 0.5 g

Diabetic Adjustment: Use gluten-free, sugar-free lemon-lime soda and ginger ale.

One serving—Calories: 61; Total fat: 1 g; Saturated fat: 0.5 g; Cholesterol: 0.5 mg; Sodium: 44 mg; Carbohydrates: 15 g; Fiber: 0 g; Sugar: 13 g; Protein: 0.5 g

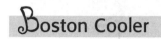 Boston Cooler

1 ½-cup scoop gluten-free vanilla ice cream

¾ cup gluten-free root beer

1 Put the ice cream into a glass.

2 Pour the root beer over the ice cream.

You can use cola or other soda in place of the root beer. Use different flavors of gluten-free ice cream.

Makes 1 1-cup serving

One serving—Calories: 215; Total fat: 3.5 g; Saturated fat: 2.5 g; Cholesterol: 15 mg; Sodium: 60 mg; Carbohydrates: 28.7 g; Fiber: 0 g; Sugar: 28.7 g; Protein: 1 g

Diabetic Adjustment: Use gluten-free, sugar-free vanilla ice cream and gluten-free, sugar-free root beer.

One serving—Calories: 57; Total fat: 3 g; Saturated fat: 2 g; Cholesterol: 13 mg; Sodium: 51 mg; Carbohydrates: 7 g; Fiber: 0 g; Sugar: 0 g; Protein: 1 g

Cherry Banana Shake

½ cup milk

½ teaspoon vanilla

1 small ripe banana, sliced

6 gluten-free maraschino cherries

1 tablespoon unsweetened cocoa

3 cups gluten-free vanilla ice cream

1 Put the milk, vanilla, banana, cherries, and cocoa in a blender.

2 Cover and, with the help of an adult, blend on high power until smooth.

3 Add ice cream. Blend at medium power until smooth. Serve immediately.

Makes 4 1-cup servings

One serving—Calories: 292; Total fat: 8 g; Saturated fat: 5.5 g; Cholesterol: 33 mg; Sodium: 122 mg; Carbohydrates: 27.8 g; Fiber: 0.5 g; Sugar: 18.6 g; Protein: 3.5 g

Diabetic Adjustment: Use skim milk in place of whole milk. Use gluten-free, sugar-free vanilla ice cream.

One serving—Calories: 107; Total fat: 3.5 g; Saturated fat: 2 g; Cholesterol: 14 mg; Sodium: 68 mg; Carbohydrates: 17.7 g; Fiber: 0.5 g; Sugar: 7.6 g; Protein: 3.3 g

Chocolate Banana Drink

½ cup chocolate milk

1 teaspoon vanilla

1 small banana, cut up

1 Put the chocolate milk, vanilla, and banana in a blender.

2 With the help of an adult, blend ingredients until smooth. Serve immediately.

For a thinner drink, add 1 or 2 ice cubes to the blender in step 1.

Makes 1 1-cup serving

One serving—Calories: 224; Total fat: 5 g; Saturated fat: 2.5 g; Cholesterol: 15 mg; Sodium: 75 mg; Carbohydrates: 41 g; Fiber: 4 g; Sugar: 11.5 g; Protein: 5 g

Milk-Free Adjustment: In place of the chocolate milk, use chocolate soy milk.

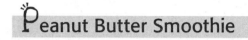

Peanut Butter Smoothie

> 1 cup gluten-free creamy peanut butter
> ¼ cup gluten-free chocolate syrup
> 1 teaspoon honey
> ¼ cup milk
> 8 ice cubes

1. Put the peanut butter, chocolate syrup, honey, milk, and ice in a blender.
2. With the help of an adult, blend until smooth. Pour into glasses.

Makes 2 1-cup servings

One serving—Calories: 843; Total fat: 65 g; Saturated fat: 9 g; Cholesterol: 9 mg; Sodium: 507 mg; Carbohydrates: 37 g; Fiber: 8 g; Sugar: 22 g; Protein: 37.5 g

Milk-Free Adjustment: Use soy milk in place of the milk.

Chocolate Soda

> 1 cup gluten-free chocolate ice cream, softened
> 3 tablespoons gluten-free chocolate syrup
> 2 cups club soda

1. Spoon the ice cream into a tall glass. Add the chocolate syrup.
2. Slowly pour in the club soda. Use a tall spoon to stir the mixture.

Makes 3 1-cup servings

One serving—Calories: 193; Total fat: 4.6 g; Saturated fat: 3.3 g; Cholesterol: 20 mg; Sodium: 83 mg; Carbohydrates: 35.6 g; Fiber: 0 g; Sugar: 33.3 g; Protein: 1.3 g

Diabetic Adjustment: Use gluten-free, sugar-free ice cream. Use sugar-free club soda.

One serving—Calories: 88; Total fat: 2 g; Saturated fat: 0 g; Cholesterol: 9 mg; Sodium: 41 mg; Carbohydrates: 17 g; Fiber: 0 g; Sugar: 14 g; Protein: 0.0 g

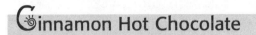 Cinnamon Hot Chocolate

1 ounce gluten-free semisweet chocolate

1 3-inch cinnamon sticks

1 cup milk

1. Using a grater, shave the chocolate. (Be careful not to scrape your fingers against the grater.)
2. Put the chocolate and cinnamon sticks in a heatproof mug.
3. Pour the milk into a small saucepan. Have an adult help you heat the milk on the stove, just to a simmer.
4. Pour the milk into the mug. Stir until the chocolate has melted.

Makes 1 1-cup serving

One serving—Calories: 286; Total fat: 16.5 g; Saturated fat: 10 g; Cholesterol: 35 mg; Sodium: 123 mg; Carbohydrates: 29.9 g; Fiber: 1.7 g; Sugar: 27.4 g; Protein: 9.2 g

Milk-Free Adjustment: Use soy milk in place of the milk.

Peach Slush

½ cup milk

1 cup canned juice-packed, sliced peaches, drained

1 teaspoon sugar

¼ teaspoon vanilla

1 Pour the milk into an ice-cube tray. Freeze for 1½ hours or until solid.

2 Put the peaches, sugar, and vanilla into a blender. Add the frozen milk.

3 With an adult's help, blend the mixture until smooth.

4 Pour the "slush" into glasses. Serve immediately.

Makes 2 6-ounce servings

One serving—Calories: 153; Total fat: 1.8 g; Saturated fat: 1.2 g; Cholesterol: 8 mg; Sodium: 40 mg; Carbohydrates: 35 g; Fiber: 3 g; Sugar: 33 g; Protein: 3.4 g

Diabetic Adjustment: Use skim milk in place of whole milk. Use brown sugar substitute in place of the sugar.

One serving—Calories: 124; Total fat: 0 g; Saturated fat: 0 g; Cholesterol: 1 mg; Sodium: 42 mg; Carbohydrates: 31 g; Fiber: 3 g; Sugar: 27 g; Protein: 3.4 g

Milk-Free Adjustment: Use soy milk in place of the milk.

Mint Lemon Fizz

2 cups cold water

⅔ cup fresh lemon juice (juice from 2 lemons)

⅓ cup sugar

4 fresh mint leaves

4 cups cold gluten-free lemon-lime soda or ginger ale

1 Pour the water into a large pitcher.

2 Pour the lemon juice through a strainer into the pitcher.

3 Stir in the sugar until completely dissolved.

4 Stir in the mint leaves.

5 Leave the pitcher on the counter for 30 minutes to let the flavors blend.

6 Remove the mint leaves.

7 Pour in the soda or ginger ale.

8 Put some ice cubes into each glass; pour the drink over the ice.

You can use fresh lime juice in place of the lemon juice.

Makes 7 1-cup servings

One serving—Calories: 53; Total fat: 0 g; Saturated fat: 0 g; Cholesterol: 0 mg; Sodium: 10 mg; Carbohydrates: 13 g; Fiber: 0 g; Sugar: 12 g; Protein: 0 g

Diabetic Adjustment: Use a sugar substitute in place of the sugar. Use gluten-free diet soda in place of the soda or ginger ale.

One serving—Calories: 17; Total fat: 0 g; Saturated fat: 0 g; Cholesterol: 0 mg; Sodium: 75 mg; Carbohydrates: 6 g; Fiber: 0 g; Sugar: 0 g; Protein: 0 g

Raspberry Cooler

1 cup orange juice

1 cup frozen raspberries

1 tablespoon confectioners' sugar

1 cup crushed ice

1 Put the orange juice, raspberries, sugar, and ice in a blender.

2 Cover and, with the help of an adult, mix at low speed until the berries are liquefied. Serve immediately.

Makes 3 1-cup servings

One serving—Calories: 70; Total fat: 0.3 g; Saturated fat: 0 g; Cholesterol: 0 mg; Sodium: 0 mg; Carbohydrates: 8 g; Fiber: 3 g; Sugar: 12 g; Protein: 0.7 g

Pineapple Berry Cooler

1 cup strawberries

1 cup pineapple chunks, fresh or canned

½ cup raspberries

3 tablespoons frozen lemonade concentrate, thawed

1 Wash berries, remove stems, and cut in half.

2 Put the strawberries, pineapple, raspberries, and lemonade concentrate in a blender.

3 With the help of an adult, blend until smooth.

4 Put a few ice cubes in a glass. Pour in the cooler.

Makes 2 1-cup servings

One serving—Calories: 170; Total fat: 3 g; Saturated fat: 0 g; Cholesterol: 0 mg; Sodium: 3 mg; Carbohydrates: 37 g; Fiber: 10 g; Sugar: 5 g; Protein: 3 g

Apple-Cranberry Punch

2 quarts apple juice

2 quarts cranberry juice

1 cup lemon juice

1 cup sugar

2 2-liter bottles ginger ale

1 Mix the apple juice, cranberry juice, lemon juice, and sugar in a punch bowl.

2 Twenty minutes before serving, add ice cubes and ginger ale.

Makes 28 1-cup servings

One serving—Calories: 276; Total fat: 0 g; Saturated fat: 0 g; Cholesterol: 0 mg; Sodium: 73 mg; Carbohydrates: 67.7 g; Fiber: 0 g; Sugar: 65.8 g; Protein: 0 g

Diabetic Adjustment: Omit the lemon juice and sugar. Use sugar-free ginger ale.

One serving—Calories: 142; Total fat: 0 g; Saturated fat: 0 g; Cholesterol: 0 mg; Sodium: 71 mg; Carbohydrates: 35.4 g; Fiber: 0 g; Sugar: 34.3 g; Protein: 0 g

Pineberry Drink

¼ cup chilled pineapple juice

¼ cup chilled orange juice

¼ cup chilled cranberry juice

1 Put a few ice cubes into an 8-ounce glass.

2 Pour the pineapple, orange, and cranberry juices into the glass. Stir to blend.

Makes 1 6-ounce serving

One serving—Calories: 100; Total fat: 0 g; Saturated fat: 0 g; Cholesterol: 0 mg; Sodium: 12 mg; Carbohydrates: 27 g; Fiber: 0 g; Sugar: 26.5 g; Protein: 0.5 g

Cranberry Punch

4 cups cranberry juice

1 ½ cups sugar

4 cups pineapple juice

1 cup orange juice

1 tablespoon almond extract

2 quarts ginger ale

1 Combine the cranberry juice, sugar, pineapple juice, and orange juice in a 1½ gallon pitcher. Stir until the sugar is dissolved. Put the pitcher in the refrigerator for 2 hours to chill.

2 Pour the juice mixture into a punch bowl. Add the ginger ale just before serving. Add ice to keep the punch cold.

Makes 17 1-cup servings

One serving—Calories: 96; Total fat: 0 g; Saturated fat: 0 g; Cholesterol: 0 mg; Sodium: 13 mg; Carbohydrates: 23 g; Fiber: 0 g; Sugar: 23 g; Protein: 0 g

Diabetic Adjustment: Omit the sugar.

One serving—Calories: 53; Total fat: 0 g; Saturated fat: 0 g; Cholesterol: 0 mg; Sodium: 12 mg; Carbohydrates: 13 g; Fiber: 0 g; Sugar: 13 g; Protein: 0 g

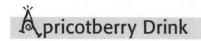pricotberry Drink

  1 15-ounce can juice-packed apricot halves

  1 10-ounce package frozen raspberries

  2 tablespoons honey

1 Drain apricot halves in a sieve.

2 Put frozen raspberries, honey, and apricot halves in a blender.

3 Have an adult help you blend the ingredients until they are smooth.

Makes 4 ¾-cup servings

One serving—Calories: 134; Total fat: 0.1 g; Saturated fat: 0 g; Cholesterol: 0 mg; Sodium: 4 mg; Carbohydrates: 34.8 g; Fiber: 4.1 g; Sugar: 30 g; Protein: 0.8 g

Diabetic Adjustment: Use unsweetened raspberries. Use brown sugar substitute in place of the honey.

One serving—Calories: 66; Total fat: 0.5 g; Saturated fat: 0 g; Cholesterol: 0 mg; Sodium: 3 mg; Carbohydrates: 12.3 g; Fiber: 5.6 g; Sugar: 9.7 g; Protein: 1.2 g

3

Breads

Cheesy Muffins

2¼ cups Gluten-Free Flour Mixture (See the Hints chapter.)

¼ teaspoon salt

4 teaspoons gluten-free baking powder

¼ teaspoon garlic powder

¾ cup sugar

5 tablespoons grated gluten-free Parmesan cheese

2 teaspoons dried dill weed

2 eggs

1 tablespoon gluten-free mayonnaise

1 cup milk

¼ cup corn oil

3 tablespoons grated gluten-free cheddar cheese

1 Preheat oven to 400°F. Spray muffin cups with gluten-free nonstick spray.

2 Put the flour mixture, salt, baking powder, garlic powder, and sugar into a sieve, and sift into a large mixing bowl. Stir in the Parmesan cheese and dill.

③ In a small bowl, whisk together the eggs, mayonnaise, milk, and oil.

④ Make a hole in the middle of the dry ingredients. Pour in the egg mixture. Stir into the dry ingredients just until evenly moistened. Spoon the batter into the greased muffin cups, filling the cups three-quarters full.

⑤ Bake for 18 to 20 minutes. Have an adult remove the muffin tins from the oven. Top each muffin with 1 teaspoon grated cheddar cheese. With help from an adult, put the muffins back in the oven for 2 minutes to melt the cheese.

Makes 20 muffins

One muffin—Calories: 115; Total fat: 4 g; Saturated fat: 1 g; Cholesterol: 45 mg; Sodium: 46 mg; Carbohydrates: 14 g; Fiber: 0.4 g; Sugar: 5 g; Protein: 3 g

Diabetic Adjustment: Use 1 whole egg and 2 egg whites for the 2 eggs. Use brown sugar substitute for the sugar. Omit the mayonnaise. Use 1% milk in place of whole milk. Omit the cheddar cheese.

One muffin—Calories: 84; Total fat: 3 g; Saturated fat: 0.7 g; Cholesterol: 11 mg; Sodium: 38 mg; Carbohydrates: 10 g; Fiber: 0.4 g; Sugar: 1 g; Protein: 2 g

Strawberry Muffins

2 10-ounce packages frozen strawberries, thawed

4 eggs

1¼ cups milk

2 teaspoons vanilla

1 tablespoon gluten-free mayonnaise

4 tablespoons butter, melted

1½ cups Gluten-Free Flour Mixture (See the Hints chapter.)

3 teaspoons gluten-free baking powder

2 teaspoons baking soda

½ teaspoon salt

¼ cup plus 1 tablespoon sugar, separated

1 Preheat oven to 375°F.

2 Put the strawberries in a strainer, and drain off juice. Cut the berries into smaller pieces. Place them in a small bowl, sprinkle with 1 tablespoon sugar, and toss gently to mix. Set the bowl aside.

3 Break the eggs into a large bowl. Add the milk, vanilla, mayonnaise, and melted butter. Whisk ingredients together about 20 times.

4 Sift the flour mixture, baking powder, baking soda, salt, and ¼ cup of sugar into the bowl with the eggs. Stir with a whisk until everything is blended. Stir in the strawberries.

5 Spray gluten-free nonstick spray into muffin tins. Spoon the muffin batter into the muffin tins, filling each tin two-thirds full. Bake for 15 minutes or until a toothpick inserted in the center of a muffin comes out clean. Have an adult remove the muffins from the oven. Remove the muffins from the tins, and let them cool on a wire rack.

Instead of the strawberries, you can use peach slices or pitted cherries.

Makes 20 muffins

One muffin—Calories: 93; Total fat: 4.3 g; Saturated fat: 0.6 g; Cholesterol: 40 mg; Sodium: 75 mg; Carbohydrates: 11.5 g; Fiber: 0.7 g; Sugar: 3.9 g; Protein: 2.4 g

Diabetic Adjustment: Use 2 whole eggs and 4 egg whites in place of the 4 whole eggs. Use skim milk in place of whole milk. Omit the mayonnaise. Use gluten-free, low-fat margarine in place of the butter. Use sugar substitute in place of the sugar.

One muffin—Calories: 73; Total fat: 2.3 g; Saturated fat: 0.6 g; Cholesterol: 22 mg; Sodium: 92 mg; Carbohydrates: 9.4 g; Fiber: 0.7 g; Sugar: 1.8 g; Protein: 3.4 g

Milk-Free Adjustment: Use soy milk in place of the milk. Omit the mayonnaise. Use gluten-free, milk-free margarine in place of the butter.

Pineapple Coconut Muffins

2 eggs
1 cup gluten-free sour cream
1 cup sugar
6 tablespoons pineapple preserves
1 tablespoon corn oil
2 teaspoons vanilla
1 tablespoon gluten-free mayonnaise
1 cup Gluten-Free Flour Mixture
    (See the Hints chapter.)
1½ teaspoons gluten-free baking powder
1 teaspoon baking soda
¼ teaspoon salt
¼ cup shredded coconut

1 Preheat oven to 350°F.
2 In a large bowl, whisk the eggs slightly.
3 Whisk in the sour cream, sugar, preserves, corn oil, vanilla, and mayonnaise.
4 Sift the flour mixture, baking powder, baking soda, and salt over the egg mixture. Stir just until ingredients are blended.
5 Stir in the coconut.

6 Spray muffin tins with gluten-free nonstick spray. Fill each muffin tin about two-thirds full with batter.

7 Bake for 20 minutes or till a toothpick inserted in the center of a muffin comes out clean.

8 Have an adult remove the hot tins from the oven. Remove the muffins from the tins, and let them cool on a wire rack.

Makes 16 muffins

One muffin—Calories: 122; Total fat: 4 g; Saturated fat: 2.7 g; Cholesterol: 19 mg; Sodium: 53 mg; Carbohydrates: 18.5 g; Fiber: 0.4 g; Sugar: 5.6 g; Protein: 1.7 g

Diabetic Adjustment: Use gluten-free, fat-free sour cream. Use brown sugar substitute in place of the white sugar. In place of the pineapple preserves, use 4 tablespoons of all-fruit preserves. Omit the mayonnaise. Use unsweetened coconut.

One muffin—Calories: 85; Total fat: 3.8 g; Saturated fat: 2.1 g; Cholesterol: 16 mg; Sodium: 48 mg; Carbohydrates: 10 g; Fiber: 0.4 g; Sugar: 4 g; Protein: 1.6 g

Milk-Free Adjustment: In place of the sour cream, use water. Use gluten-free, milk-free margarine in place of the butter. Omit the mayonnaise.

Peanut Butter Banana Muffins

2 eggs

2 egg whites

½ cup mashed banana (about 2 bananas, mashed with a fork)

1 cup 1% milk

¼ cup gluten-free peanut butter

⅓ cup corn oil

1 teaspoon vanilla

2 tablespoons honey

¼ cup brown sugar

¼ cup frozen apple juice concentrate, thawed

¼ cup nonfat dry milk

2¼ cups Gluten-Free Flour Mixture (See the Hints chapter.)

3 teaspoons gluten-free baking powder

1½ teaspoons baking soda

1 Preheat oven to 350°F.

2 Put the eggs and egg whites in a large bowl. Use a whisk to beat them a little bit.

3 Stir the mashed banana, milk, peanut butter, corn oil, vanilla, honey, brown sugar, apple juice concentrate, and dry milk into the eggs. Mix with a spoon until the mixture is creamy.

4 Sift the flour mixture, baking powder, and baking soda over the egg mixture. Stir until blended.

5 Line muffin tins with paper liners or lightly spray them with gluten-free nonstick spray. Spoon in the muffin batter, filling each muffin cup two-thirds full.

6 Bake 15 minutes or until a toothpick inserted in the center of a muffin comes out clean.

7 Have an adult remove the muffin tins from the oven. Remove the muffins from the tins, and let them cool on a wire rack.

You can put a small dollop of jelly on top of each muffin before baking.

Makes 18 muffins

One muffin—Calories: 326; Total fat: 12 g; Saturated fat: 2.2 g; Cholesterol: 39 mg; Sodium: 81 mg; Carbohydrates: 31 g; Fiber: 2 g; Sugar: 9.6 g; Protein: 8 g

Diabetic Adjustment: Use brown sugar substitute for the brown sugar.

One muffin—Calories: 260; Total fat: 12 g; Saturated fat: 2.2 g.; Cholesterol: 39 mg; Sodium: 80 mg; Carbohydrates: 29 g; Fiber: 2 g; Sugar: 6 g; Protein: 8 g

Harvest Muffins

½ cup chopped prunes

1 cup chopped dates

½ cup raisins

1 ¼ cups water

¼ cup gluten-free, low-fat margarine

¼ teaspoon salt

½ cup unsweetened applesauce

½ cup orange juice

¼ cup olive oil

3 eggs, slightly beaten

1 teaspoon vanilla

1 teaspoon almond extract

½ cup chopped nuts

1 ½ cups Gluten-Free Flour Mixture (See the Hints chapter.)

1 ½ teaspoons baking soda

½ teaspoon cinnamon

1. Preheat oven to 350°F.
2. Put the prunes, dates, and raisins in a large saucepan. Add the water, and bring to a boil on the stove. Boil for 5 minutes.
3. Add the margarine and salt. Stir until margarine is melted. Remove the pan from the stove, and let mixture cool.
4. Stir in the applesauce, orange juice, olive oil, eggs, vanilla, almond extract, and nuts. Lightly whip with a fork.
5. Sift the flour mixture, baking soda, and cinnamon over the fruit mixture. Stir just until the batter is evenly moist. Spray muffin tins with gluten-free nonstick spray. Spoon the batter into the muffin tins, filling each muffin cup two-thirds full.
6. Bake for 15 minutes or until a toothpick inserted in the center of a muffin comes out clean.
7. Have an adult help you remove the hot tins from the oven. Carefully remove the hot muffins from the tins. Let them cool on a wire rack.

Makes 16 muffins

One muffin—Calories: 167; Total fat: 8.7 g; Saturated fat: 1.5 g; Cholesterol: 40 mg; Sodium: 86 mg; Carbohydrates: 21 g; Fiber: 1.3 g; Sugar: 6.3 g; Protein: 3.1 g

Milk-Free Adjustment: Use gluten-free, milk-free margarine.

Chocolate Pumpkin Muffins

3 eggs

1 tablespoon gluten-free mayonnaise

1¼ cups canned pumpkin

½ cup butter, melted

½ cup pecans, chopped

¾ cup semisweet chocolate chips

1⅔ cups Gluten-Free Flour Mixture (See the Hints chapter.)

1 cup sugar

½ teaspoon gluten-free baking powder

2 teaspoons baking soda

1 tablespoon gluten-free pumpkin pie spice

¼ teaspoon salt

1. Preheat oven to 350°F.
2. Break the eggs into a large bowl. Whisk them until frothy.
3. Add the mayonnaise, pumpkin, and butter. Whisk until blended.
4. Stir the pecans and chocolate chips into the egg mixture.
5. Sift the flour mixture, sugar, baking powder, baking soda, pumpkin pie spice, and salt over the egg mixture. Stir the batter just until blended.
6. Spray muffin tins with gluten-free nonstick spray. Fill each tin two-thirds full with batter.
7. Bake for 18 minutes or until a toothpick inserted in the center of a muffin comes out clean. Have an adult help remove

the hot tins from the oven, then remove the muffins from tins and place on cooling racks.

Makes 20 muffins

One muffin—Calories: 142; Total fat: 7.3 g; Saturated fat: 2 g; Cholesterol: 36 mg; Sodium: 60 mg; Carbohydrates: 23.4 g; Fiber: 0.9 g; Sugar: 14.8 g; Protein: 2.1 g

Diabetic Adjustment: Use 2 whole eggs and 2 egg whites in place of the 3 eggs. Omit the mayonnaise. Use gluten-free, fat-free margarine in place of the butter. Omit the chocolate chips. Use brown sugar substitute in place of the sugar.

One muffin—Calories: 84; Total fat: 4.9 g; Saturated fat: 1.2 g; Cholesterol: 24 mg; Sodium: 69 mg; Carbohydrates: 8.1 g; Fiber: 0.9 g; Sugar: 0.7 g; Protein: 2.1 g

Milk-Free Adjustment: Omit the mayonnaise. Use gluten-free, milk-free margarine in place of the butter.

Milk-Free Carrot Bread

1 ½ cups grated carrots

⅓ cup sugar

3 eggs

½ teaspoon salt

⅔ cup corn oil

1 teaspoon vanilla

¾ teaspoon cinnamon

¾ teaspoon gluten-free
    baking powder

¾ teaspoon baking soda

1 ½ cups Gluten-Free Flour Mixture (See the Hints chapter.)

½ cup raisins

1 Preheat oven to 350°F.

2 In a large bowl, stir together the carrots, sugar, eggs, salt, corn oil, and vanilla.

③ Place a sieve over the bowl. Pour the cinnamon, baking powder, baking soda, and flour mixture into the sieve, and sift over the carrot mixture.

④ With a spoon, stir in the raisins until all ingredients are blended.

⑤ Spray a 9″ × 5″ × 3″ loaf pan with gluten-free nonstick spray. Pour the batter into the loaf pan.

⑥ Bake for 50 minutes or until a toothpick inserted near the center of the loaf comes out clean. Have an adult help you remove the hot pan from the oven. Let it cool on a wire rack.

Try making carrot muffins by baking this batter in muffin tins for 30 minutes. Makes 16 muffins.

Makes 1 loaf (12 slices)

One slice—Calories: 190; Total fat: 10 g; Saturated fat: 1 g; Cholesterol: 53 mg; Sodium: 122 mg; Carbohydrates: 21 g; Fiber: 1 g; Sugar: 9 g; Protein: 2.7 g

Diabetic Adjustment: Use brown sugar substitute for the white sugar. Use 2 whole eggs and 2 egg whites in place of the 3 eggs. Instead of the ⅔ cup corn oil, use ¼ cup corn oil and ¼ cup pineapple juice.

One slice—Calories: 136; Total fat: 5.5 g; Saturated fat: 0.6 g; Cholesterol: 35 mg; Sodium: 119 mg; Carbohydrates: 18 g; Fiber: 1 g; Sugar: 6 g; Protein: 2.7 g

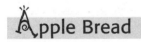

Apple Bread

¾ cup corn oil

⅓ cup applesauce

1 cup brown sugar

4 eggs

2 teaspoons vanilla

1 tablespoon gluten-free mayonnaise

1¾ cups chopped apples (peeled and cored)

½ cup chopped walnuts

1 tablespoon grated orange zest

1½ cups Gluten-Free Flour Mixture (See the Hints chapter.)

1 tablespoon baking soda

¼ teaspoon salt

2 teaspoons cinnamon

½ teaspoon nutmeg

1. Preheat oven to 350°F.
2. In a large bowl, whisk together the corn oil, applesauce, and brown sugar.
3. Add the eggs, vanilla, and mayonnaise. Whisk until blended. Stir in the apples, walnuts, and orange zest.
4. Sift the flour mixture, baking soda, salt, cinnamon, and nutmeg over the apple mixture. Stir batter just until blended.
5. Spray a 9″ × 5″ × 3″ loaf pan with gluten-free nonstick spray. Pour the batter into the pan.
6. Bake for 55 minutes or until a toothpick inserted in the center comes out clean. Have an adult help you remove the hot pan from the oven.
7. Let the pan set for 10 minutes, then turn it upside down to remove the loaf. Let the loaf cool on a wire rack.

Makes 1 loaf (14 slices)

One slice—Calories: 245; Total fat: 15.7 g; Saturated fat: 2.1 g; Cholesterol: 61 mg; Sodium: 61 mg; Carbohydrates: 22.9 g; Fiber: 0.9 g; Sugar: 11.5 g; Protein: 3.8 g

Diabetic Adjustment: Use unsweetened applesauce. Use brown sugar substitute in place of the brown sugar. Use 2 whole eggs and 4 egg whites in place of the 4 eggs. Omit the walnuts.

One slice—Calories: 179; Total fat: 12.5 g; Saturated fat: 1.7 g; Cholesterol: 30 mg; Sodium: 70 mg; Carbohydrates: 15 g; Fiber: 0.7 g; Sugar: 1.2 g; Protein: 3.3 g

Corn Bread

2 eggs

1 cup milk

¼ cup corn oil

1 tablespoon gluten-free mayonnaise

1 cup cornmeal

1 cup Gluten-Free Flour Mixture (See the Hints chapter.)

3 teaspoons gluten-free baking powder

¾ teaspoon salt

2 tablespoons sugar

½ cup drained canned corn

1. Preheat oven to 400°F.
2. Break the eggs into a large bowl. Whip with a whisk. Add the milk, corn oil, and mayonnaise; whip with a whisk.
3. Stir in cornmeal.
4. Put the flour mixture, baking powder, salt, and sugar in a strainer. Sift over the egg mixture. Beat batter with a wooden spoon until smooth. Stir in the corn.
5. Spray an 8-inch square baking pan with gluten-free nonstick spray. Pour the batter into the pan.
6. Bake for 25 minutes or until a toothpick inserted in the center comes out clean.
7. Have an adult remove the hot pan from the oven and place it on a rack to cool.

Makes 9 squares

One square—Calories: 174; Total fat: 9.6 g; Saturated fat: 1.8 g; Cholesterol: 52 mg; Sodium: 252 mg; Carbohydrates: 17 g; Fiber: 0.8 g; Sugar: 3 g; Protein: 4.2 g

Diabetic Adjustment: Use 1 egg and 2 egg whites in place of the 2 eggs. Use 1% milk in place of whole milk. Omit the mayonnaise. Use brown sugar substitute for the sugar. Use canned corn that has no salt added.

One square—Calories: 157; Total fat: 8 g; Saturated fat: 1.3 g; Cholesterol: 25 mg; Sodium: 238 mg; Carbohydrates: 15.7 g; Fiber: 0.8 g; Sugar: 1.8 g; Protein: 4.2 g

Milk-Free Adjustment: Use soy milk in place of the milk. Omit the mayonnaise.

Cheese Bread

½ cup warm water

1 packet (2¼ tablespoons) gluten-free dry yeast

3 eggs

2 egg whites

⅓ cup olive oil

2 tablespoons gluten-free mayonnaise

½ cup grated gluten-free Romano cheese

1½ cups Gluten-Free Flour Mixture (See the Hints chapter.)

2 tablespoons sugar

¼ teaspoon salt

1 teaspoon pepper

1 teaspoon ground oregano

½ teaspoon garlic powder

½ teaspoon dried dill weed

¾ cup shredded gluten-free sharp cheddar cheese

1 In a small bowl, sprinkle the yeast over the water. Let it set for a few minutes to soften.

2 In a large bowl, whip the eggs and egg whites well with a whisk until very frothy. Stir in the yeast and water, olive oil, mayonnaise, and Romano cheese.

③ Sift the flour mixture and sugar together over the egg mixture. Add the salt, pepper, oregano, garlic powder, and dill. Stir well to mix.

④ Spray a 10″ tube pan with gluten-free nonstick spray. Pour half of the batter into the pan. Sprinkle the cheddar cheese over the batter in the pan. Pour in the rest of the batter to cover the cheese.

⑤ Spray one side of a piece of waxed paper with gluten-free nonstick spray. Cover the pan with the waxed paper, greased side down, facing the dough. Lay a dish towel over the waxed paper. Set the bowl on the counter, away from any drafts, and let the dough rest and rise for 2 hours.

⑥ Preheat the oven to 325°F.

⑦ Remove the towel and waxed paper. Bake the loaf for about 30 minutes or until the bread sounds hollow when tapped lightly on top. (Have an adult help you check for doneness and remove the hot pan from the oven.)

Makes 1 loaf (16 slices)

One slice—Calories: 171; Total fat: 11.5 g; Saturated fat: 4.4 g; Cholesterol: 58 mg; Sodium: 183 mg; Carbohydrates: 10.3 g; Fiber: 0.5 g; Sugar: 1.2 g; Protein: 7.5 g

Pumpkin Bread

2 cups Gluten-Free Flour Mixture (See the Hints chapter.)

4 teaspoons gluten-free baking powder

1 teaspoon baking soda

½ teaspoon salt

1½ teaspoons cinnamon

½ teaspoon nutmeg

3 eggs

1¼ cups canned pumpkin

1 cup sugar

2 tablespoons molasses

½ cup corn oil

2 teaspoons vanilla

½ cup water

1 tablespoon gluten-free mayonnaise

¾ cup coarsely chopped pecans

3 ounces gluten-free cream cheese, cut into 16 small cubes

1 Preheat oven to 350°F.

2 Sift the flour mixture, baking powder, baking soda, salt, cinnamon, and nutmeg into a medium-size bowl.

3 Break the eggs into a larger bowl. Beat with a whisk until the eggs are blended. Add the pumpkin, sugar, molasses, corn oil, vanilla, water, and mayonnaise. Stir well.

4 Fold in the dry ingredients, stirring until smooth. If using pecans, stir them in now.

5 Spray a 9″ × 5″ × 3″ loaf pan with gluten-free nonstick spray. Pour the batter into the loaf pan. Place the cream cheese cubes in a row down the center of the batter.

6 Bake for 45 to 55 minutes, until a toothpick inserted in the center of the loaf comes out clean.

7 Have an adult remove the bread from the oven and set it on a cooling rack. After 10 minutes, turn the pan over and remove the bread. Let the bread cool completely.

Makes 1 loaf (16 slices)

One slice—Calories: 173; Total fat: 8.3 g; Saturated fat: 1.1 g; Cholesterol: 40 mg; Sodium: 94 mg; Carbohydrates: 22.1 g; Fiber: 1.1 g; Sugar: 9.7 g; Protein: 2.5 g

Diabetic Adjustment: Use 1 whole egg and 4 egg whites in place of the 3 eggs. Use brown sugar substitute in place of the sugar. Omit the mayonnaise. Omit the cream cheese.

One slice—Calories: 132; Total fat: 7 g; Saturated fat: 0.9 g; Cholesterol: 13 mg; Sodium: 93 mg; Carbohydrates: 14.6 g; Fiber: 1.1 g; Sugar: 2.1 g; Protein: 2.5 g

Milk-Free Adjustment: Omit the mayonnaise. Omit the cream cheese.

Cheese Pretzels

For a birthday party, you can make pretzels in the shape of your age or the letters of your name!

¾ cup warm water

1 package (2¼ tablespoons) gluten-free dry yeast

½ teaspoon salt

2¼ tablespoons sugar

2 cups Gluten-Free Flour Mixture (See the Hints chapter.)

¾ cup grated gluten-free cheddar cheese

1 egg, beaten

1 Preheat oven to 425°F.

2 In a large bowl, sprinkle the yeast over the water. Let it soak 5 minutes to soften.

3 Sift ¼ teaspoon salt, the sugar, and the flour mixture over the yeast. Stir in the cheese. Sprinkle your hands with a little flour mixture, then knead the dough well. (Kneading is folding the dough over and over. This works air into the dough to make it lighter.)

4 Lightly spray a cookie sheet with gluten-free nonstick spray. Divide the dough into 18 equal-sized balls. Roll each ball into a worm shape, then form pretzels, alphabet letters, numbers, or other shapes. Place each shape on the greased cookie sheet.

5 Beat the egg lightly in a small bowl. Brush the tops of the pretzels with the beaten egg, and sprinkle lightly with the remaining ¼ teaspoon of salt.

Bake for 15 minutes. Have an adult remove the hot cookie sheet from the oven. Use a spatula to place pretzels on a wire rack to cool.

Makes 18 pretzels

One pretzel—Calories: 90; Total fat: 3 g; Saturated fat: 1.7 g; Cholesterol: 45 mg; Sodium: 219 mg; Carbohydrates: 11 g; Fiber: 0.6 g; Sugar: 0 g; Protein: 4 g

Diabetic Adjustment: Replace the sugar with brown sugar substitute. Use low-fat or nonfat cheese. Use 2 egg whites in place of the egg.

One pretzel—Calories: 65; Total fat: 1 g; Saturated fat: 0 g; Cholesterol: 3 mg; Sodium: 168 mg; Carbohydrates: 10 g; Fiber: 0.6 g; Sugar: 0 g; Protein: 1 g

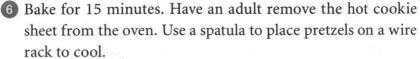

Sesame Crackers

> 2 cups Gluten-Free Flour Mixture (See the Hints chapter.)
> ½ teaspoon salt
> ¼ cup brown sugar
> ⅓ cup corn oil
> ¼ cup unsweetened apple juice
> 1 cup sesame seeds

1. Preheat oven to 325°F.
2. Sift the flour mixture, salt, and brown sugar into a medium mixing bowl.
3. Stir in the corn oil and juice until all is moistened.
4. Add the sesame seeds. Mix thoroughly by hand.
5. With a rolling pin, roll out the dough on a surface floured using additional gluten-free flour mixture. Roll the dough to ½-inch thickness.
6. Cut into 2-inch squares.
7. Lightly spray a baking sheet with gluten-free nonstick spray. Place the crackers on the baking sheet.

8 Poke the top of each cracker in two different places with a fork.

9 Bake 20 to 25 minutes, until the edges brown. Have an adult help you remove the baking sheet from the oven. Let the crackers cool on a wire rack.

Makes about 60 crackers

One cracker: Calories: 38; Total fat: 2.3 g; Saturated fat: 0 g; Cholesterol: 0 mg; Sodium: 20 mg; Carbohydrates: 3 g; Fiber: 0.2 g; Sugar: 0.7 g; Protein: 1 g

Diabetic Adjustment: Use brown sugar substitute in place of the brown sugar. Omit the salt.

One cracker—Calories: 36; Total fat: 2.3 g; Saturated fat: 0.3 g; Cholesterol: 0 mg; Sodium: 1 mg; Carbohydrates: 3.3 g; Fiber: 0.2 g; Sugar: 0.3 g; Protein: 0.9 g

4

Breakfasts

Blueberry Coffee Cake

2 eggs

½ cup milk

½ cup gluten-free low-fat vanilla yogurt

3 tablespoons corn oil

1 teaspoon vanilla

2 cups Gluten-Free Flour Mixture (See the Hints chapter.)

½ cup sugar

6 teaspoons gluten-free baking powder

½ teaspoon salt

¼ teaspoon cinnamon

1½ cups blueberries

Topping

3 tablespoons sugar

¼ teaspoon cinnamon

2 tablespoons chopped nuts (optional)

1. Preheat oven to 350°F.
2. Break the eggs into a large bowl. Add the milk, yogurt, corn oil, and vanilla. Mix well with a whisk.
3. Sift the flour mixture, sugar, baking powder, salt, and cinnamon over the egg mixture. Stir just until blended.
4. Spray a 9-inch square pan with gluten-free nonstick spray. Spread the batter in the pan. Sprinkle the blueberries on top of the batter.
5. For the topping, stir together the sugar, cinnamon, and nuts (if desired) in a small bowl. Sprinkle over top of batter.
6. Bake for 35 minutes or until a toothpick inserted in the center of the coffee cake comes out clean.
7. Have an adult remove the pan from the oven and set it on a rack to cool.

Makes 9 3-inch-square servings

One serving—Calories: 210; Total fat: 6.8 g; Saturated fat: 1 g; Cholesterol: 49 mg; Sodium: 160 mg; Carbohydrates: 34 g; Fiber: 1.4 g; Sugar: 13 g; Protein: 5 g

Diabetic Adjustment: Use 1 whole egg and 2 egg whites in place of the 2 eggs. Use 1% milk in place of whole milk. Use ¼ cup pear juice plus ¼ cup brown sugar substitute in place of the sugar in the cake. Omit the sugar from the topping.

One serving—Calories: 167; Total fat: 5 g; Saturated fat: 0.8 g; Cholesterol: 24 mg; Sodium: 162 mg; Carbohydrates: 25 g; Fiber: 1.4 g; Sugar: 6 g; Protein: 5 g

Peachy Breakfast Cake

4 eggs

5 ounces gluten-free bread (about 4 slices)

1 teaspoon vanilla

1 teaspoon cinnamon

1 teaspoon baking soda

2 tablespoons corn oil

1 15¼-ounce can sliced peaches, packed in juice

⅓ cup sugar

⅓ cup raisins

⅓ cup chopped walnuts

Cinnamon

1. Preheat oven to 350°F.
2. Break the eggs into a blender. Tear the bread into tiny pieces, and add to the eggs.
3. Add the vanilla, cinnamon, baking soda, and corn oil. Drain and discard ½ cup of the peach juice. Add the remaining peach juice and the peaches and sugar to the blender. With the help of an adult, blend the ingredients until smooth.
4. Spray an 8-inch square pan with gluten-free nonstick spray. Pour the batter into the pan.
5. Stir in the raisins and nuts. Sprinkle the top with cinnamon. Bake for 40 minutes or until a knife inserted in the center of the cake comes out clean. Have an adult help you remove the hot pan from the oven. Cut into squares and serve warm.

Makes 6 2- by 3-inch servings

One serving—Calories: 271; Total fat: 11.3 g; Saturated fat: 2 g; Cholesterol: 141 mg; Sodium: 101 mg; Carbohydrates: 37 g; Fiber: 3.3 g; Sugar: 28.8 g; Protein: 7 g

Diabetic Adjustment: Use 2 eggs and 4 egg whites in place of the 4 eggs. Use brown sugar substitute in place of the sugar called for in the recipe. Omit the raisins.

One serving—Calories: 205; Total fat: 9.6 g; Saturated fat: 1.5 g; Cholesterol: 71 mg; Sodium: 115 mg; Carbohydrates: 24.3 g; Fiber: 2.8 g; Sugar: 16.8 g; Protein: 7 g

Milk-Free Adjustment: Use gluten-free, milk-free bread.

Layered Breakfast Casserole

1 10-ounce bag gluten-free frozen hash brown potatoes

¾ pound gluten-free sausage links

6 eggs

1 cup milk

1 tablespoon dried parsley flakes

6 ounces gluten-free sharp cheddar cheese, grated

1 large tomato

¼ teaspoon salt

¼ teaspoon pepper

1 Preheat oven to 350°F.

2 Spray a 9-inch square pan with gluten-free nonstick spray. Line the bottom of the pan with the hash brown potatoes.

3 Put the sausage in a shallow glass dish. Poke each sausage twice with a fork. Microwave on High for 4 minutes.

4 Remove the sausage from the microwave. Drain on paper towels.

5 Cut the sausage into little pieces, about the size of small grapes. Sprinkle the sausage pieces on top of the hash browns.

6 In a medium bowl, whisk together the eggs, milk, and parsley. Pour the egg mixture over the sausage.

7 Sprinkle the grated cheese on top of the egg mixture.

8 Cut the tomato into thin slices. Lay the slices on top of the cheese. Sprinkle the tomato with the salt and pepper.

9 Bake for 55 minutes. Have an adult help you remove the hot pan from the oven.

Makes 6 2- by 3-inch servings

One serving—Calories: 519; Total fat: 36.8 g; Saturated fat: 16.3 g; Cholesterol: 302 mg; Sodium: 861 mg; Carbohydrates: 18 g; Fiber: 0.5 g; Sugar: 3.5 g; Protein: 25 g

Milk-Free Adjustment: Use soy milk in place of the milk. Omit the cheese.

Night-Before Oven French Toast

If any French toast is left over, you may heat it up the next day in the toaster.

6 eggs
3 tablespoons sugar
1 teaspoon cinnamon
1 cup milk
1 teaspoon vanilla
8 slices gluten-free bread

1. Spray a cookie sheet with gluten-free nonstick spray, or grease the cookie sheet with a little soft butter.
2. Break the eggs into a wide bowl. Add the sugar, cinnamon, milk, and vanilla. Use a wire whisk to beat the mixture until it is well blended.
3. Dip each bread slice into the mixture, pushing the bread down so it is covered with egg mix. Place the bread on the greased cookie sheet.
4. After all the bread slices have been dipped, pour any remaining liquid evenly over them. Cover the cookie sheet with plastic wrap. Refrigerate it for 6 hours or overnight.
5. The next morning, preheat oven to 350°F.
6. Bake the French toast for 10 minutes. Have an adult remove the cookie sheet from the oven with pot holders. Turn over

each piece of toast. Have the adult return the cookie sheet to the oven to bake for another 10 minutes, or until the toast is lightly browned. If desired, top with jelly, maple syrup, or fresh strawberries, or sprinkle with sugar.

Makes 4 2-slice servings

One serving—Calories: 225; Total fat: 11 g; Saturated fat: 2 g; Cholesterol: 226 mg; Sodium: 268 mg; Carbohydrates: 20 g; Fiber: 2 g; Sugar: 7 g; Protein: 9 g

Diabetic Adjustment: Use 4 whole eggs plus 4 egg whites in place of the 6 eggs. Use brown sugar substitute in place of the sugar. Use 1% milk in place of whole milk.

One serving—Calories: 129; Total fat: 3 g; Saturated fat: 1 g; Cholesterol: 106 mg; Sodium: 220 mg; Carbohydrates: 15 g; Fiber: 1 g; Sugar: 3 g; Protein: 8 g

Milk-Free Adjustment: Use soy milk in place of the milk.

PB&J Toasted Sandwiches

5 eggs

1½ cups milk

3 tablespoons sugar

1 tablespoon vanilla

8 slices gluten-free bread

4 tablespoons gluten-free peanut butter

4 tablespoons jelly

1 large banana

2 teaspoons corn oil

1 In a shallow bowl, whisk the eggs slightly. Add the milk, sugar, and vanilla. Whisk again.

2 Spread one side of each of 4 slices of bread with a thin layer of peanut butter. Spread the jelly over the peanut butter layers. Cut the banana into 16 slices. Lay 4 slices on each sandwich on top of the jelly. Put the 4 remaining slices of bread on top of the banana layers to form four sandwiches.

3 Preheat a large, nonstick skillet or griddle on the stove for 1 minute. With a pastry brush, lightly brush the pan with the corn oil.

4 Soak one sandwich at a time in the egg mixture, carefully turning it over one time, until very wet.

5 Working in batches if necessary, have an adult help you place the soaked sandwiches in the skillet or on the griddle. Cook the sandwiches, turning them once with a spatula, until they are golden on both sides.

Makes 4 sandwiches

One sandwich—Calories: 515; Total fat: 21.2 g; Saturated fat: 5.2 g; Cholesterol: 278 mg; Sodium: 289 mg; Carbohydrates: 61.3 g; Fiber: 3.2 g; Sugar: 26.9 g; Protein: 20.2 g

Diabetic Adjustment: Use 3 eggs and 4 egg whites in place of the 5 eggs. Use 1% milk. Use brown sugar substitute in place of the sugar. Use all-fruit jelly. Serving size: ½ sandwich.

One sandwich—Calories: 235; Total fat: 7.8 g; Saturated fat: 2.1 g; Cholesterol: 88 mg; Sodium: 206 mg; Carbohydrates: 28 g; Fiber: 1.6 g; Sugar: 10.7 g; Protein: 10.4 g

Milk-Free Adjustment: Use soy milk in place of the milk. Use gluten-free, milk-free bread.

Breakfast Blueberry Pudding

1 tablespoon butter, melted

4 eggs

⅓ cup sifted Gluten-Free Flour Mixture (See the Hints chapter.)

2 teaspoons vanilla

1 cup milk

¼ cup honey

½ teaspoon salt

½ teaspoon cinnamon

⅔ cup blueberries (fresh or frozen)

1. Preheat oven to 400°F.
2. Put the melted butter, eggs, flour mixture, vanilla, milk, honey, salt, and cinnamon into a blender. With an adult's help, blend the mixture until smooth.
3. Spray a 9-inch square pan with gluten-free nonstick spray. Pour the mixture into the pan.
4. Gently stir in the blueberries.
6. Bake for 20 to 25 minutes, or until puffed and golden. Have an adult help you take the hot pan from the oven.
7. To serve, cut into squares. If desired, drizzle maple syrup over each piece before serving.

Makes 9 3-inch-square servings

One serving—Calories: 110; Total fat: 4.5 g; Saturated fat: 1.2 g; Cholesterol: 101 mg; Sodium: 186 mg; Carbohydrates: 13.7 g; Fiber: 0.4 g; Sugar: 9.6 g; Protein: 4.2 g

Diabetic Adjustment: Use gluten-free, low-fat margarine in place of the butter. Use 2 whole eggs and 4 egg whites in place of the 4 eggs. Use 1% milk in place of whole milk. Use brown sugar substitute in place of the honey.

One serving—Calories: 63; Total fat: 2.1 g; Saturated fat: 0.6 g; Cholesterol: 48 mg; Sodium: 201 mg; Carbohydrates: 6.2 g; Fiber: 0.4 g; Sugar: 2.6 g; Protein: 4.4 g

Milk-Free Adjustment: Use gluten-free, milk-free margarine in place of the butter. Use soy milk in place of the milk.

Night-Before Breakfast Casserole

1¼ cups milk

4 eggs

¾ teaspoon vanilla

½ teaspoon cinnamon

¼ teaspoon salt

8 slices gluten-free bread

4 slices gluten-free American cheese

4 thin slices gluten-free ham

½ cup gluten-free cornflakes

2 tablespoons butter

1. In a medium bowl, whisk together the milk, eggs, vanilla, cinnamon, and salt.
2. Generously spray a 9-inch square pan with gluten-free nonstick spray. Pour one-third of the egg mixture into the bottom of the pan.
3. Cut the crusts from the bread and discard. Place 4 slices of bread in the pan.
4. Lay 1 slice of cheese and 1 slice of ham on each piece of bread in the pan. Top with the 4 remaining bread slices. Pour the remaining egg mixture over the bread in the pan.
5. Cover with plastic wrap. Refrigerate for at least 8 hours (so the bread absorbs the moisture).
6. Preheat oven to 350°F.
7. Put the cornflakes in a plastic bag, and crush them with a rolling pin. Transfer the crumbs to a small bowl. Melt the butter in a glass measuring cup in the microwave. Pour the

melted butter over the cornflakes, and mix to blend. Sprinkle the cereal mixture over the top of the casserole.

8 Bake uncovered for 40 minutes. Have an adult help you remove the hot pan from the oven. If desired, serve with maple syrup.

Makes 4 4½-inch-square servings

One serving—Calories: 467; Total fat: 26 g; Saturated fat: 9.1 g; Cholesterol: 270 mg; Sodium: 1,357 mg; Carbohydrates: 32 g; Fiber: 2.8 g; Sugar: 7.6 g; Protein: 25.3 g

am and Egg Cups

4 medium slices gluten-free ham
1 small tomato
4 eggs
Dash salt
Dash pepper

1 Preheat oven to 350°F.

2 Spray four custard cups with gluten-free nonstick spray. Put a round slice of ham in the bottom and up the sides of each cup.

3 Cut the tomato into 4 slices. Place 1 tomato slice on top of each piece of ham. Break an egg into each cup. Sprinkle lightly with salt and pepper.

4 Bake for 15 minutes or until the egg is cooked the way you like it. Have an adult help you remove the custard cups from the oven.

Makes 4 Ham and Egg Cups

One Ham and Egg Cup—Calories: 109; Total fat: 6.2 g; Saturated fat: 2 g; Cholesterol: 218 mg; Sodium: 453 mg; Carbohydrates: 1.7 g; Fiber: 0.2 g; Sugar: 0 g; Protein: 11 g

Mashed Breakfast

This is also good spread on untoasted gluten-free bread to pack for a school lunch.

1 ripe banana, peeled
1 tablespoon gluten-free peanut butter
2 teaspoons gluten-free jelly
1 slice gluten-free bread

1. Cut the banana into several chunks. Put the banana in a sandwich-size, reclosable plastic bag. Add the peanut butter and the jelly to the bag.
2. Seal the bag securely. Have fun smooshing, mashing, and rolling the contents of the bag until they are well blended.
3. Toast the bread in the toaster. Spread your "banana mash" on the toast.

Makes 1 breakfast

One breakfast—Calories: 314; Total fat: 10 g; Saturated fat: 1 g; Cholesterol: 0 mg; Sodium: 210 mg; Carbohydrates: 51 g; Fiber: 5 g; Sugar: 9 g; Protein: 9 g

Breakfast Quiche

4 eggs
1 10-ounce box frozen chopped broccoli, thawed
1 medium potato
1 small onion
1 cup grated gluten-free cheddar cheese
6 slices gluten-free bacon
¼ teaspoon salt
¼ teaspoon pepper
¼ teaspoon dried dill weed

1 Preheat oven to 350°F.

2 Whisk the eggs in a medium bowl until frothy.

3 Squeeze the broccoli dry, then add it to the bowl.

4 Shred the potato, onion, and cheese (watch your fingers!). Add the shredded potato, onion, and cheese to the broccoli.

5 Lay the bacon on a microwave-safe dish, and cover it with a paper towel. Microwave on High for 5 minutes or until the bacon is crisp. Use a fork to transfer the bacon from the dish to a paper towel. (The bacon will be very hot.) Let the bacon drain on the paper towel. When the bacon has cooled a little, break it into small chunks and add it to the bowl.

6 Stir in the salt, pepper, and dill.

7 Pour the mixture into a 9-inch pie plate.

8 Bake for 45 minutes or until a knife inserted in the center comes out clean. Have an adult help you remove the quiche from the oven. Let the quiche rest for 5 minutes, then cut into wedges.

Makes 6 wedges

One wedge—Calories: 191; Total fat: 12.8 g; Saturated fat: 6.2 g; Cholesterol: 166 mg; Sodium: 366 mg; Carbohydrates: 7 g; Fiber: 0.8 g; Sugar: 1 g; Protein: 12 g

Eggs in a Bottle

8 eggs

½ cup milk

⅛ teaspoon salt

⅛ teaspoon pepper

¼ teaspoon dehydrated
   minced onion flakes

½ teaspoon dried parsley flakes

¼ cup shredded gluten-free cheddar cheese

1 tablespoon butter

1. Break the eggs into a large measuring cup. Pour the eggs into a 1-quart widemouthed jar with a lid.
2. Add the milk, salt, pepper, onion, parsley, and cheese to the jar.
3. Screw the lid onto the jar tightly.
4. Shake the jar until all of the ingredients are mixed and the eggs look frothy.
5. Have an adult melt the butter over medium heat in a 10-inch nonstick skillet.
6. Carefully pour the eggs into the skillet.
7. Have an adult help you use a wooden spoon to stir the eggs gently until they are set.

In place of the cheddar cheese, try using Swiss, provolone, feta, or gluten-free American cheese.

Makes 5 2-egg (approximately) servings

One serving—Calories: 180; Total fat: 13 g; Saturated fat: 4.2 g; Cholesterol: 354 mg; Sodium: 229 mg; Carbohydrates: 2.2 g; Fiber: 0 g; Sugar: 2.4 g; Protein: 12.2 g

Breakfast Enchiladas

These tortillas are excellent topped with a little gluten-free sour cream.

4 gluten-free corn tortillas

4 slices gluten-free ham

1¼ cups grated gluten-free sharp cheddar cheese

¼ cup chopped green onions

½ cup chopped green pepper

3 eggs

1 cup milk

¼ cup gluten-free salsa

2 teaspoons cornstarch

⅛ teaspoon salt

⅛ teaspoon black pepper

⅛ teaspoon red pepper flakes

1 Preheat oven to 350°F.

2 Wrap the tortillas in foil. Bake for 5 minutes to soften them.

3 Lay out the tortillas. Lay 1 slice of ham on each tortilla. Sprinkle one-quarter of the cheese on each tortilla.

4 Place one-quarter of the onion and green pepper pieces on each tortilla.

5 Spray a 9-inch square baking dish with gluten-free nonstick spray. Roll up each tortilla and place it, seam side down, in the dish.

6 In a medium bowl, mix the eggs, milk, salsa, cornstarch, salt, pepper, and red pepper flakes with a fork. Pour the egg mixture over the tortillas.

7 Spray one side of a 12-inch square piece of foil with gluten-free nonstick spray. Cover the baking dish with the foil, sprayed side down. Bake for 35 minutes. Have an adult help you remove the foil, then continue to bake for another 10 minutes. Have an adult help you remove the hot pan from the oven.

Makes 4 enchiladas

One enchilada—Calories: 402; Total fat: 25.5 g; Saturated fat: 10 g; Cholesterol: 256 mg; Sodium: 543 mg; Carbohydrates: 23.5 g; Fiber: 1.2 g; Sugar: 3.5 g; Protein: 21 g

Banana Pancakes

1 tablespoon butter

1 ripe banana

2 eggs

¾ teaspoon vanilla

1¼ cups milk

¾ cup Gluten-Free Flour Mixture (See the Hints chapter.)

1 tablespoon sugar

¼ teaspoon cinnamon

2 teaspoons gluten-free baking powder

¼ teaspoon salt

1. Have an adult melt the butter in a small saucepan.
2. In a medium-size bowl, mash the banana with a fork. Whisk the eggs, vanilla, milk, and melted butter into the banana until well mixed.
3. Sift the flour mixture, sugar, cinnamon, baking powder, and salt over the bowl with the egg mixture. Whisk the batter until smooth. Let mixture sit for 10 minutes.
4. Spray a large skillet or griddle with gluten-free nonstick spray. Have an adult set the skillet or griddle on the stove to preheat. Using a ¼ cup or small ladle, spoon the batter into the pan.
5. With the help of an adult, cook the pancakes over medium heat until small bubbles appear on top. Gently turn them over, using a spatula, and let them cook till the bottoms are lightly browned.

For extra fun, add two small circles of batter near the top of each pancake to form the head of Mickey Mouse!

Makes 4 3-pancake servings

One serving—Calories: 213; Total fat: 7.7 g; Saturated fat: 1.9 g; Cholesterol: 122 mg; Sodium: 239 mg; Carbohydrates: 28.5 g; Fiber: 1.5 g; Sugar: 5.2 g; Protein: 2.5 g

Diabetic Adjustment: Use brown sugar substitute for the sugar. Use gluten-free, salt-free margarine in place of the butter. Use skim milk in place of whole milk.

One serving—Calories: 184; Total fat: 4.9 g; Saturated fat: 1.2 g; Cholesterol: 11 mg; Sodium: 247 mg; Carbohydrates: 27 g; Fiber: 1.5 g; Sugar: 3.7 g; Protein: 2.5 g

Milk-Free Adjustment: Use gluten-free, milk-free margarine in place of the butter. Use soy milk in place of the milk.

Cottage Cheese Pancakes

These pancakes are excellent when served with maple syrup or jam.

4 eggs

1 cup gluten-free cottage cheese

1 tablespoon butter, melted

½ teaspoon vanilla

¼ cup Gluten-Free Flour Mixture (See the Hints chapter.)

½ teaspoon gluten-free baking powder

2½ teaspoons sugar

¼ teaspoon salt

¼ teaspoon cinnamon

1. Put the eggs, cottage cheese, butter, and vanilla in a blender. With the help of an adult, blend for 10 seconds.
2. Sift the flour mixture, baking powder, sugar, salt, and cinnamon into the blender. Place the lid on top, then blend until smooth.
3. Have an adult help you warm a griddle or large skillet. Lightly spray the griddle or skillet with gluten-free nonstick spray. Using a meat baster, squeeze about ¼-cup pancake batter onto the hot griddle or skillet and cook until bubbles appear around the sides. Turn each pancake over, and continue to cook until the bottoms are lightly browned.

Makes 3 3-pancake servings

One serving—Calories: 204; Total fat: 11.6 g; Saturated fat: 2.7 g; Cholesterol: 298 mg; Sodium: 449 mg; Carbohydrates: 10.6 g; Fiber: 0.3 g; Sugar: 4.5 g; Protein: 13.7 g

Diabetic Adjustment: Use 3 whole eggs and 2 egg whites in place of the 4 eggs. Use gluten-free, low-fat cottage cheese. Use 2 teaspoons gluten-free, low-fat margarine in place of the butter. Use brown sugar substitute in place of the sugar.

One serving—Calories: 168; Total fat: 7.3 g; Saturated fat: 2.3 g; Cholesterol: 212 mg; Sodium: 447 mg; Carbohydrates: 9.3 g; Fiber: 0.3 g; Sugar: 1.7 g; Protein: 15 g

Cornmeal Pancakes

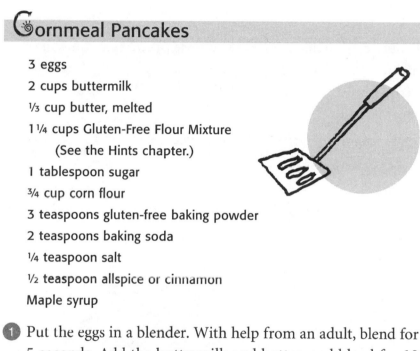

3 eggs

2 cups buttermilk

⅓ cup butter, melted

1¼ cups Gluten-Free Flour Mixture
    (See the Hints chapter.)

1 tablespoon sugar

¾ cup corn flour

3 teaspoons gluten-free baking powder

2 teaspoons baking soda

¼ teaspoon salt

½ teaspoon allspice or cinnamon

Maple syrup

❶ Put the eggs in a blender. With help from an adult, blend for 5 seconds. Add the buttermilk and butter, and blend for 10 seconds.

❷ Sift the flour mixture into the blender, then add the sugar, corn flour, baking powder, baking soda, salt, and allspice or cinnamon. Blend the batter for 1 minute, stopping the blender every 20 seconds to scrape the sides.

❸ Spray a large skillet or griddle with gluten-free nonstick spray. With an adult's help, preheat the pan or griddle on the stove. When it is hot, use a baster or ladle to spoon about ½-cup batter into the pan.

4 When bubbles appear around the edges, have an adult help you turn them over so they brown on the other side. Repeat until you have used all the batter. Serve with maple syrup.

Makes 5 2-pancake servings

One serving (without maple syrup)—Calories: 345; Total fat: 17 g; Saturated fat: 1 g; Cholesterol: 157 mg; Sodium: 331 mg; Carbohydrates: 37.4 g; Fiber: 2 g; Sugar: 2.2 g; Protein: 10.8 g

Diabetic Adjustment: Use 2 whole eggs and 2 egg whites in place of the 3 eggs. Use low-fat buttermilk. Use gluten-free, low-fat margarine in place of the butter. In place of the sugar, use brown sugar substitute.

One serving (without maple syrup)—Calories: 306; Total fat: 13.2 g; Saturated fat: 3.7 g; Cholesterol: 185 mg; Sodium: 376 mg; Carbohydrates: 36 g, Fiber: 1.6 g; Sugar: 1 g; Protein: 11.6 g

Milk-Free Adjustment: Use soy milk in place of the buttermilk.

5

Main Dishes

Spaghetti Pie

½ pound uncooked gluten-free spaghetti

1 tablespoon olive oil

2 cups gluten-free spaghetti sauce

½ cup grated gluten-free Parmesan cheese

¼ teaspoon red pepper flakes

½ teaspoon dried basil

¾ teaspoon ground oregano

¼ teaspoon garlic powder

1 tablespoon dried parsley flakes

½ cup grated gluten-free mozzarella cheese

1 Preheat oven to 350°F. Break the dry spaghetti noodles into smaller pieces (roughly into thirds). In a large pot of boiling water, cook the spaghetti al dente (just barely tender). Have an adult help you heat the water and drain the spaghetti into a colander.

2 Pour the olive oil into a 9-inch pie plate. Use a pastry brush to spread it on the bottom and sides of the pan.

③ Put the spaghetti into a large bowl. Pour the spaghetti sauce over the spaghetti.

④ Sprinkle the Parmesan cheese, red pepper flakes, basil, oregano, garlic powder, and parsley over the spaghetti. Stir spaghetti with a fork to mix everything evenly.

⑤ Pour the spaghetti into the pie plate. With the back of a spoon, pat it down. Sprinkle the top with the mozzarella cheese.

⑥ Bake for 30 minutes. Have an adult help you remove the hot dish from the oven. Cut the pie into six wedges to serve.

Makes 6 wedges

One wedge—Calories: 168; Total fat: 9 g; Saturated fat: 2.3 g; Cholesterol: 10 mg; Sodium: 736 mg; Carbohydrates: 14.3 g; Fiber: 3.3 g; Sugar: 4 g; Protein: 7.1 g

Spaghetti Pizza

8 ounces gluten-free spaghetti

1 egg

¼ cup milk

¼ teaspoon salt

½ teaspoon garlic powder

¾ cup plus 2 tablespoons shredded gluten-free
     mozzarella cheese

2 tablespoons grated gluten-free sharp cheddar cheese

¼ cup grated gluten-free Romano cheese

1 15-ounce jar gluten-free spaghetti sauce

¾ teaspoon ground oregano

½ teaspoon dried basil

6 ounces gluten-free Romano cheese, grated

1 8-ounce can sliced mushrooms, drained

2 ounces gluten-free sliced pepperoni

1. Preheat oven to 400°F.
2. Break spaghetti into 2-inch pieces. Have an adult help you cook the spaghetti al dente (just barely tender) in boiling water as package directs. Drain, then cool spaghetti.
3. In a large bowl, use a whisk to beat the egg till frothy. Stir in the milk, salt, garlic powder, 2 tablespoons of mozzarella cheese, the cheddar cheese, and ¼ cup of Romano cheese. Add the cooked spaghetti to the egg mixture. Stir well with a fork.
4. Spray a small pizza pan with gluten-free nonstick spray. Spread the spaghetti in the pan evenly. Bake for 10 minutes. Have an adult remove the pan from the oven. Reduce the oven temperature to 350°F.
5. Spread the spaghetti sauce evenly over the spaghetti. (The pan will be hot, so hold it with a pot holder.) Sprinkle the oregano, basil, and remaining mozzarella and Romano cheeses over the top. Top with mushrooms and pepperoni slices.
6. Have an adult help you return the pan to the oven. Bake the pizza for 15 minutes more. Let stand at room temperature for 5 minutes. Cut into 6 slices.

Makes 6 slices

One slice—Calories: 361; Total fat: 15.6 g; Saturated fat: 3.7 g; Cholesterol: 54 mg; Sodium: 934 mg; Carbohydrates: 35 g; Fiber: 3 g; Sugar: 5.1 g; Protein: 21.4 g

Tuna Melt

1 6½-ounce can water-packed tuna, drained
1 rib celery, diced
2 tablespoons minced green pepper
1 green onion, minced
¼ cup gluten-free mayonnaise
4 slices gluten-free bread
4 thin slices tomato
¼ cup grated gluten-free cheddar cheese

1 Preheat broiler.

2 In a small bowl, stir together the tuna, celery, green pepper, onion, and mayonnaise until well mixed.

3 Place the bread slices on a broiler pan.

4 With a knife, spread one-fourth of the tuna mixture on each piece of bread.

5 Place a slice of tomato on top of each sandwich.

6 Sprinkle one-fourth (1 tablespoon) of the cheese on top of each sandwich.

7 Have an adult help you broil the sandwiches about 3 minutes, or just until the tops begin to bubble and are golden.

Makes 4 sandwiches

One sandwich—Calories: 288; Total fat: 17 g; Saturated fat: 5.2 g; Cholesterol: 27 mg; Sodium: 482 mg; Carbohydrates: 14.1 g; Fiber: 1.4 g; Sugar: 2.1; Protein: 18.4 g

Diabetic Adjustment: Use gluten-free, low-fat mayonnaise. In place of the cheddar cheese, use gluten-free part-skim mozzarella cheese.

One sandwich—Calories: 227; Total fat: 9.5 g; Saturated fat: 1.5 g; Cholesterol: 8 mg; Sodium: 520 mg; Carbohydrates: 15.6 g; Fiber: 1.5 g; Sugar: 3.1 g; Protein: 18.5 g

Parmesan Fish

Excellent choices of fish for this dish are whitefish, flounder, scrod, cod, and orange roughy.

⅓ cup gluten-free cornflakes

⅓ cup grated gluten-free Parmesan cheese

¼ teaspoon basil

¼ teaspoon paprika

¼ teaspoon pepper

¼ teaspoon salt

1 tablespoon dried parsley flakes

1 tablespoon butter

1 tablespoon lemon juice

1 pound firm fish fillets, about ½ inch thick

1 Preheat oven to 450°F.

2 Put the cornflakes in a sandwich-size, reclosable plastic bag. With a rolling pin, crush the flakes. Put the crushed flakes into a small bowl.

3 With a fork, stir in the Parmesan cheese, basil, paprika, pepper, salt, and parsley.

4 Have an adult help you melt the butter in a small pan. Stir the lemon juice into the melted butter.

5 Pour the butter mixture over the crumbs in the bowl. Blend well with a fork until the crumbs are evenly moistened.

6 Place the fish in a single layer in a greased shallow baking dish. Pat the crumbs onto the top of the fish.

7 Bake for 10 minutes or until the fish flakes easily with a fork.

Makes 4 ¼-pound servings

One serving (with cod fillets)—Calories: 158; Total fat: 5.8 g; Saturated fat: 1.2 g; Cholesterol: 44 mg; Sodium: 379 mg; Carbohydrates: 6.5 g; Fiber: 0.7 g; Sugar: 1.2 g; Protein: 16.2 g

Tuna à la Pie

½ cup cooked rice

1 tablespoon dried parsley flakes

2 tablespoons melted gluten-free margarine

2 teaspoons dried onion flakes

2 eggs

1 6½-ounce can water-packed tuna, drained

½ cup frozen peas

¼ cup sliced canned mushrooms

2 tablespoons chopped pimiento (optional)

¾ cup shredded gluten-free sharp cheddar cheese

3 tablespoons gluten-free, low-fat mayonnaise

⅓ cup milk

½ teaspoon paprika

1. Preheat oven to 350°F.
2. In a medium bowl, use a fork to mix together the rice, parsley, margarine, 1 teaspoon of onion flakes, and 1 egg.
3. Using the back of the fork, press the rice mixture on the bottom and up the sides of a 9-inch pie plate that has been sprayed with gluten-free nonstick spray.
4. Put the remaining egg in the bowl used to mix the rice. Whisk it until frothy.
5. Add the remaining 1 teaspoon of onion flakes and the tuna, peas, mushrooms, pimiento, cheese, mayonnaise, milk, and paprika. Stir well.
6. Spoon the tuna mixture into the pie shell.
7. Bake for 45 minutes or until a knife inserted in the center comes out clean.
8. Have an adult help you remove the hot plate from the oven. Cut into 5 wedges.

Makes 5 wedges

One wedge—Calories: 320; Total fat: 17.6 g; Saturated fat: 7.7 g; Cholesterol: 119 mg; Sodium: 466 mg; Carbohydrates: 19.2 g; Fiber: 0.6 g; Sugar: 3.8 g; Protein: 21 g

Meat Loaf Muffins

½ cup warm water

1 gluten-free beef bouillon cube

1 cup gluten-free cornflake crumbs

1 pound ground beef

1 teaspoon salt

¼ teaspoon pepper

2 tablespoons dried parsley flakes

2 tablespoons dried onion flakes

¼ teaspoon garlic powder

1 egg

1 teaspoon gluten-free Worcestershire sauce

2 tablespoons brown sugar

¼ cup gluten-free ketchup

1. Preheat oven to 350°F.
2. Pour water over bouillon in a large bowl. Let the bouillon soak for 2 minutes.
3. Add the cornflake crumbs, ground beef, salt, pepper, parsley, onion flakes, garlic powder, egg, and Worcestershire sauce. With your hands (washed just before and afterward), blend the mixture well.
4. Spray muffin tins with gluten-free nonstick spray. Divide the meat mixture into six portions; pack into muffin tins.
5. Bake for 20 minutes.
6. While the meat loaves are baking, stir together the brown sugar and ketchup in a small bowl.
7. Have an adult help you remove the tins from the oven. Spoon the ketchup mixture evenly over the top of the meat. Return the tins to the oven, and bake for 20 minutes more.

Makes 6 Meat Loaf Muffins

One Meat Loaf Muffin—Calories: 244; Total fat: 14 g; Saturated fat: 5.5 g;
Cholesterol: 97 mg; Sodium: 682 mg; Carbohydrates: 9.4 g; Fiber: 0.3 g; Sugar:
5.5 g; Protein: 19 g

Diabetic Adjustment: Use 2 egg whites in place of the egg. Omit
the topping of brown sugar and ketchup.

One Meat Loaf Muffin—Calories: 219; Total fat: 13.1 g; Saturated fat: 5.1 g;
Cholesterol: 62 mg; Sodium: 584 mg; Carbohydrates: 4.2 g; Fiber: 0.2 g; Sugar:
0.5 g; Protein: 19.5 g

Taco Casserole

- 1 pound lean ground beef
- 1 medium onion, chopped
- 3 cups crushed gluten-free tortilla chips
- 1 packet gluten-free mild taco seasoning mix
- 1 16-ounce can whole tomatoes (undrained)
- 1 cup gluten-free sour cream
- 1 cup shredded gluten-free cheddar cheese

1. Crumble the ground beef into a microwave-safe pan. Mix in the onion. Microwave the meat on High, uncovered, for 3 minutes. Remove the pan, and break up pieces of meat with a fork. Return the meat to the microwave and cook 3 minutes more, until browned. Drain the meat.

2. Spray a 9-inch square microwave-safe casserole with gluten-free nonstick spray. Layer 1 cup of the tortilla chips in the bottom of the casserole.

3. Spread the ground beef over the chips. Sprinkle the taco seasoning mix over the beef.

4. Spread the tomatoes over the seasoning mix.

5. Spread the sour cream on top of the tomatoes.

6. Sprinkle the cheese over the sour cream.

7. Top with the remaining tortilla chips.

⑧ Microwave the casserole on High, uncovered, for 3 minutes, then rotate the dish. Microwave for 3 more minutes or until cheese melts and casserole is heated through. If more cooking time is needed, rotate the dish again before continuing. The dish may be hot, so use a pot holder to rotate it and to remove it from the oven.

Makes 6 2- by 3-inch servings

One serving—Calories: 446; Total fat: 30.6 g; Saturated fat: 13.3 g; Cholesterol: 94 mg; Sodium: 639 mg; Carbohydrates: 16.6 g; Fiber: 1.6 g; Sugar: 2.8 g; Protein: 25.3 g

Diabetic Adjustment: Use 2 cups of tortilla chips instead of 3 cups. Use salt-free canned tomatoes. Use gluten-free, fat-free sour cream. In place of the cheddar cheese, substitute ½ cup shredded gluten-free cheddar cheese plus ½ cup shredded gluten-free, low-fat mozzarella cheese.

One serving—Calories: 368; Total fat: 20.6 g; Saturated fat: 9.5 g; Cholesterol: 70 mg; Sodium: 506 mg; Carbohydrates: 13.3 g; Fiber: 1.3 g; Sugar: 2 g; Protein: 24.8 g

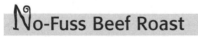 No-Fuss Beef Roast

    1 8-ounce can tomato sauce

    ¾ teaspoon salt

    ¼ teaspoon pepper

    ¼ teaspoon garlic powder

    ½ teaspoon cinnamon

    1 tablespoon dried parsley flakes

    1 tablespoon oregano

    ¼ teaspoon red pepper flakes

    2 teaspoons cornstarch

    1 cup water

    1 cube gluten-free beef bouillon

    1 pound English-cut beef roast

1 cup baby carrots

1 medium onion, sliced

1 rib celery, sliced

¼ green pepper, sliced thin

1 cup frozen peas

2 cups frozen green beans

1 Preheat oven to 350°F.

2 Cut a piece of heavy-duty foil that is a little more than double the length of a 9″ × 13″ pan. Place the foil inside the pan, letting the ends hang out.

3 In a bowl, whisk together the tomato sauce, salt, pepper, garlic powder, cinnamon, parsley, oregano, red pepper flakes, and cornstarch. In a small bowl, dissolve bouillon cube in water; whisk into tomato sauce mixture.

4 Spoon one-quarter of the sauce into the foil-lined pan.

5 Place the beef roast in the pan on top of the sauce.

6 Sprinkle the vegetables around the roast.

7 Carefully pour the remaining sauce on the roast and vegetables.

8 Bring foil overhangs up to the center, and fold them together securely. Fold the sides of the foil securely so the roast is totally sealed. Roast for 3½ hours or until the meat is very tender. Have an adult help you remove the hot pan from the oven.

Makes 4 servings (¼ pound of meat plus 1 cup of vegetables)

One serving—Calories: 288; Total fat: 5.7 g; Saturated fat: 1.7 g; Cholesterol: 89 mg; Sodium: 1,143 mg; Carbohydrates: 19.6 g; Fiber: 4.8 g; Sugar: 9.8 g; Protein: 38.2 g

Diabetic Adjustment: Use salt-free tomato sauce. Reduce salt to ¼ teaspoon. Omit the garlic powder. Omit the peas.

One serving—Calories: 255; Total fat: 5.5 g; Saturated fat: 1.7 g; Cholesterol: 89 mg; Sodium: 651 mg; Carbohydrates: 13.9 g; Fiber: 4.2 g; Sugar: 5.6 g; Protein: 36.1 g

Tortilla Tower

½ pound lean ground beef

¼ teaspoon pepper

½ teaspoon oregano

1 15-ounce jar gluten-free spaghetti sauce

1 egg

1 cup gluten-free, small-curd cottage cheese

4 gluten-free corn tortillas

1 cup shredded gluten-free sharp cheddar cheese

1. Preheat oven to 350°F.
2. With the help of an adult, brown the ground beef in a skillet. As the meat browns, break it up into tiny pieces with a fork.
3. When the meat is browned, stir in the pepper, oregano, and spaghetti sauce. Simmer the meat sauce for 5 minutes.
4. In a small bowl, whisk the egg slightly, then stir in the cottage cheese.
5. Spoon ¼ cup of the meat sauce into the bottom of a 9-inch pie plate. Place 1 tortilla on top of the sauce in the plate. Spread one-third of the cottage cheese mixture on top of the tortilla. Top with one-fourth of the remaining meat sauce, then one-fourth of the shredded cheese. Repeat layers, in this order two more times. Top with last tortilla, remaining meat sauce, and remaining shredded cheese.
6. Bake for 30 minutes. Have an adult help you remove the hot pie plate from the oven. Let stand for 5 minutes. Cut into 4 wedges to serve.

Makes 4 wedges

One wedge—Calories: 540; Total fat: 33 g; Saturated fat: 13 g; Cholesterol: 147 mg; Sodium: 1,153 mg; Carbohydrates: 26.2 g; Fiber: 3.2 g; Sugar: 6 g; Protein: 34.7 g

Dinner in a Pouch

This is also a good recipe for a camping trip.

2 large potatoes

½ green pepper

1 medium onion

¼ teaspoon salt

¼ teaspoon black pepper

1 15-ounce can corn kernels, drained

½ cup water

1 cup gluten-free ketchup

1 pound lean ground beef

1. Preheat oven to 400°F.
2. Cut four 20″ × 18″ pieces of heavy-duty foil. Fold each in half to form an 18″ × 10″ rectangle.
3. Cut the potatoes into ¾-inch cubes. Slice the green pepper and onion into thin slices. (Watch your fingers so you don't cut yourself.) In a large bowl, stir together the potatoes, green pepper, onion, salt, pepper, corn, water, and ketchup.
4. Divide the beef into four equal portions. Form a patty out of each portion. Place a beef patty in the center of each piece of foil.
5. Spoon one-fourth of the potato mixture over each beef patty.
6. Wrap each packet securely, using double-fold seals. (Allow some room for heat expansion.)
7. Place the packets on a cookie sheet. Bake for 45 minutes.

Makes 4 servings (¼ pound beef plus ½ potato and 4 ounces vegetables)

One serving—Calories: 327; Total fat: 6.5 g; Saturated fat: 2.4 g; Cholesterol: 59 mg; Sodium: 849 mg; Carbohydrates: 42.3 g; Fiber: 3.4 g; Sugar: 20.4 g; Protein: 25.7 g

Skillet Supper

1 pound lean ground beef

2 cups water

1 15-ounce jar gluten-free spaghetti sauce

1 teaspoon oregano

2 cups gluten-free elbow macaroni

½ cup shredded gluten-free mozzarella cheese

1 cup grated gluten-free Fontinella or Parmesan cheese

1 With the help of an adult, brown the ground beef in a large skillet over medium-high heat, breaking up the meat with a fork. Stir in the water, spaghetti sauce, and oregano. Bring to a simmer over medium heat.

2 Stir in the macaroni. Cover the pan, and simmer for 7 minutes until the macaroni is just cooked, stirring frequently. Stir in the cheeses. Cover the pan and let stand for 1 minute or until the cheese is completely melted.

Makes 4 2-cup servings

One serving—Calories: 456; Total fat: 22.7 g; Saturated fat: 8.9 g; Cholesterol: 69 mg; Sodium: 1,125 mg; Carbohydrates: 28 g; Fiber: 3.3 g; Sugar: 5.5 g; Protein: 32 g

Best-Ever Chili

1 tablespoon olive oil

¾ pound lean ground beef

1 large onion, chopped

½ green pepper, chopped

½ cup canned tomato sauce

¼ cup water

1 15-ounce can kidney beans (undrained)

½ teaspoon garlic powder

1 teaspoon gluten-free chili powder

¼ teaspoon cayenne

1 teaspoon unsweetened cocoa

½ teaspoon sugar

½ teaspoon salt

¼ teaspoon black pepper

¼ cup grated gluten-free Parmesan cheese

1 Heat the olive oil in a medium pot on the stove. With the help of an adult, brown the beef, onion, and green pepper in the oil, breaking up the meat with a fork.

2 Stir in the tomato sauce, water, kidney beans, garlic powder, chili powder, cayenne, cocoa, sugar, salt, and black pepper.

3 Reduce the heat to a simmer. Cover the pot, and let the chili simmer for 2½ hours.

4 Just before serving, stir in the cheese.

You may also make this chili in a slow cooker. Brown the meat, onions, and green pepper on the stove, as in step 1. Transfer the mixture to a slow cooker. Stir in the remaining ingredients, except cheese, as in step 2. Cover the pot, and cook on low heat for 8 hours. Stir in the cheese just before serving.

Makes 4 1-cup servings

One serving—Calories: 376; Total fat: 19.5 g; Saturated fat: 6.8 g; Cholesterol: 74 mg; Sodium: 738 mg; Carbohydrates: 22.6 g; Fiber: 4 g; Sugar: 3.3 g; Protein: 28 g

All-in-One Dinner

1 10-ounce box frozen chopped spinach, thawed

½ green pepper

1 onion

1 pound lean ground beef

1 15-ounce can diced tomatoes
 (undrained)

2 8-ounce cans tomato sauce

1 cup uncooked rice

¼ cup grated gluten-free Parmesan cheese

¾ teaspoon gluten-free chili powder

½ teaspoon salt

¼ teaspoon black pepper

½ cup water

1. Preheat oven to 400°F.
2. Squeeze the spinach dry. Place it in a large bowl.
3. Chop the green pepper and onion into small pieces. Add them to the bowl.
4. Sprinkle little chunks of the ground beef into the bowl.
5. Add the tomatoes, tomato sauce, rice, cheese, chili powder, salt, black pepper, and water. Stir well to blend, breaking up meat and spinach with the edge of a spoon.
6. Spray a 2-quart casserole with gluten-free nonstick spray. Place the mixture in the casserole. Pack it down lightly, and smooth the surface.
7. Cover the casserole with a lid or foil. Bake for 1¼ hours. Have an adult help you remove the hot pan from the oven.

Makes 6 1½-cup servings

One serving—Calories: 311; Total fat: 14.3 g; Saturated fat: 6 g; Cholesterol: 64 mg; Sodium: 603 mg; Carbohydrates: 22 g; Fiber: 2.1 g; Sugar: 2 g; Protein: 22.5 g

Diabetic Adjustment: Reduce rice to ½ cup. Omit the Parmesan cheese. Use salt-free tomato sauce.

One serving—Calories: 257; Total fat: 13.3 g; Saturated fat: 5.1 g; Cholesterol: 62 mg; Sodium: 278 mg; Carbohydrates: 14.6 g; Fiber: 2.1 g; Sugar: 2 g; Protein: 20.5 g

Cinnamon Rice Meatballs

1 small onion

1 pound lean ground beef

½ cup uncooked rice

½ cup plus ¼ cup water

¼ teaspoon celery salt

¼ teaspoon salt

¼ teaspoon pepper

¼ teaspoon garlic powder

¾ teaspoon dried mint flakes

1 tablespoon dried parsley flakes

½ teaspoon cinnamon

1 15-ounce can tomato sauce

1 Preheat oven to 350°F.

2 Peel off the outer skin of the onion, and throw it away. Chop the onion into very small pieces.

3 In a medium bowl, mix the onion, ground beef, rice, ½ cup of water, celery salt, salt, pepper, garlic powder, mint, and parsley. (The easiest way to mix this is with your hands.)

4 With your hands, shape the meat mixture into balls about the size of cherry tomatoes.

5 Spray an 8″ × 12″ baking pan with gluten-free nonstick spray. Place the meatballs in the pan.

6 In a small bowl, stir together the cinnamon, ¼ cup of water, and the tomato sauce. Spoon this sauce over the meatballs.

Cover the baking pan with foil. Bake for 45 minutes. With the help of an adult, uncover the hot pan and bake 15 minutes longer.

Makes 4 5-meatball servings

One serving—Calories: 376; Total fat: 19.7 g; Saturated fat: 7.7 g; Cholesterol: 93 mg; Sodium: 690 mg; Carbohydrates: 91.1 g; Fiber: 2 g; Sugar: 3.6 g; Protein: 29.2 g

Almost Cheeseburger

You can serve this meat as a dip with crackers or strips of gluten-free bread. For a hearty meal, spread it over gluten-free elbow macaroni (boiled separately).

> ½ pound lean ground beef
>
> 1 teaspoon dried onion flakes
>
> 1 pound gluten-free processed cheese, cut into cubes
>
> ¼ cup milk
>
> 1 tablespoon gluten-free ketchup
>
> 2 tablespoons gluten-free mustard

 Spray a skillet with gluten-free nonstick spray. Have an adult help you brown the beef and onion flakes in the skillet over medium-high heat, breaking up the meat with a fork as it cooks.

Lower heat and stir in the cheese, milk, ketchup, and mustard. Continue stirring until the cheese has melted.

Makes 8 ½-cup servings

One serving—Calories: 266; Total fat: 17.6 g; Saturated fat: 10.3 g; Cholesterol: 76 mg; Sodium: 924 mg; Carbohydrates: 7.5 g; Fiber: 0.1 g; Sugar: 5.4 g; Protein: 17.5 g

Corned Beef and Cabbage

4 large red-skinned potatoes, each cut into 4 wedges (about
    2 pounds)
1 2-pound corned beef brisket
8 whole black peppercorns
2 bay leaves
½ large head of cabbage

1. Place the potatoes on the bottom of a large slow cooker. Care-fully cut most of the visible fat from the corned beef. (You may need an adult to help you with this.) If the roast is too large to fit in the slow cooker, cut it into two pieces. Put the corned beef on top of the potatoes. Sprinkle the peppercorns and bay leaves on top.

2. Cut the cabbage into four wedges. (You may need an adult to help you with this.) Remove the hard center core from each wedge. Put the cabbage wedges on top of the meat. Add enough water to just barely cover the cabbage. Cook on low heat for 8 hours. Serve with gluten-free mustard, if desired. Note that corned beef shrinks to about half its original size while cooking.

Makes 4 servings (¼-pound brisket plus 1 potato and ⅛ head of cabbage)

One serving—Calories: 515; Total fat: 32.6 g; Saturated fat: 10.5 g; Cholesterol: 168 mg; Sodium: 1,939 mg; Carbohydrates: 21.1 g; Fiber: 2.4 g; Sugar: 0 g; Protein: 33 g

Slow-Cooker Steak

1 green pepper
1 rib celery
1 onion
1 pound lean round steak

2 cups gluten-free beef broth

1 tablespoon gluten-free soy sauce

1 tablespoon gluten-free Worcestershire sauce

1 tablespoon dried parsley flakes

¼ teaspoon red pepper flakes

¼ teaspoon ginger

¼ teaspoon garlic powder

½ teaspoon salt

¼ teaspoon black pepper

1. Thinly slice the green pepper, celery, and onion. Lay the vegetables in the bottom of a slow cooker.
2. Place meat on top of vegetables.
3. Stir beef broth, soy sauce, Worcestershire sauce, parsley, red pepper flakes, ginger, garlic powder, salt, and black pepper together in a bowl. When mixed, pour over meat in the slow cooker.
4. Cover the pot. Cook on low power for 9 hours.
5. To serve, have an adult help you slice the meat into thin strips.

Makes 4 ¼-pound servings

One serving—Calories: 215; Total fat: 5.5 g; Saturated fat: 1.7 g; Cholesterol: 89 mg; Sodium: 1,306 mg; Carbohydrates: 4.2 g; Fiber: 0.8 g; Sugar: 0.5 g; Protein: 35 g

Diabetic Adjustment: Use gluten-free, low-salt beef broth and soy sauce. Omit the Worcestershire sauce. Omit the garlic powder.

One serving—Calories: 211; Total fat: 5.2 g; Saturated fat: 1.7 g; Cholesterol: 89 mg; Sodium: 807 mg; Carbohydrates: 3.7 g; Fiber: 0.8 g; Sugar: 0.2 g; Protein: 35 g

Slow-Cooker Sausage

1 pound gluten-free smoked sausage

1 onion, chopped

½ teaspoon oregano

1 15-ounce jar gluten-free spaghetti sauce

1 Cut the sausage into ½-inch slices. Put the sausage, chopped onion, oregano, and spaghetti sauce in a slow cooker.

2 Cover and cook on low heat for 6 hours.

Makes 4 1-cup servings

One serving—Calories: 430; Total fat: 32 g; Saturated fat: 11.2 g; Cholesterol: 92 mg; Sodium: 1,660 mg; Carbohydrates: 8.7 g; Fiber: 2.2 g; Sugar: 4.5 g; Protein: 24.5 g

Baked Ham Slices

6 4-ounce slices gluten-free ham

2 tablespoons honey

2 tablespoons brown sugar

¼ cup water

1 Preheat oven to 350°F.

2 Spray an 8″ × 12″ baking dish with gluten-free nonstick spray. Put the ham slices in the dish.

3 Drizzle the honey over the ham.

4 Sprinkle the brown sugar over the ham.

5 Pour the water around the ham (not on top of the ham).

6 Cover the pan with foil. Bake for 30 minutes.

7 Have an adult help you remove the hot pan from the oven.

Makes 6 ¼-pound servings

One serving—Calories: 175; Total fat: 5.7 g; Saturated fat: 1.8 g; Cholesterol: 33 mg; Sodium: 1,287 mg; Carbohydrates: 5.8 g; Fiber: 0 g; Sugar: 5.1 g; Protein: 24 g

Diabetic Adjustment: Use brown sugar substitute in place of the honey and brown sugar.

One serving—Calories: 155; Total fat: 5.7 g; Saturated fat: 1.8 g; Cholesterol: 33 mg; Sodium: 1,287 mg; Carbohydrates: 0.5 g; Fiber: 0 g; Sugar: 0 g; Protein: 24 g

Slow-Cooker Pork Chops

6 6-ounce pork chops

½ teaspoon garlic powder

3 tablespoons gluten-free soy sauce

½ cup gluten-free Italian dressing

1 18-ounce bottle gluten-free barbecue sauce

1. Wash the pork chops under cold running water. Pat dry with paper towels.
2. Sprinkle the garlic powder on both sides of the chops.
3. Place the chops in a large quart-size, reclosable plastic bag.
4. Pour in the soy sauce and the Italian dressing.
5. Seal the bag securely. Push the bag around gently to distribute the marinade between the chops.
6. Refrigerate the meat in the bag for 3 or more hours.
7. Remove the pork chops from the marinade, and place them in a slow cooker.
8. Pour the barbecue sauce over the chops, lifting the chops with a fork to distribute the sauce evenly.
9. Cover the pot. Cook on low heat for 8 hours.

Makes 6 pork chops

One pork chop—Calories: 460; Total fat: 25.9 g; Saturated fat: 7 g; Cholesterol: 73 mg; Sodium: 2,089 mg; Carbohydrates: 32 g; Fiber: 0 g; Sugar: 25.4 g; Protein: 23.6 g

Diabetic Adjustment: Omit the marinade (soy sauce, Italian dressing, and garlic powder). Use only 1½ cups of the bottle of barbecue sauce.

One pork chop—Calories: 314; Total fat: 14.6 g; Saturated fat: 5 g; Cholesterol: 73 mg; Sodium: 902 mg; Carbohydrates: 20.6 g; Fiber: 0 g; Sugar: 16.8 g; Protein: 22.6 g

Country Ribs

2 pounds lean country-style pork ribs

¾ cup maple syrup

⅓ cup applesauce

3 tablespoons gluten-free ketchup

1 tablespoon gluten-free Worcestershire sauce

2 tablespoons lemon juice

¼ teaspoon salt

¼ teaspoon pepper

¼ teaspoon garlic powder

¼ teaspoon cinnamon

1 Lay the ribs in a slow cooker.

2 In a bowl, stir together the maple syrup, applesauce, ketchup, Worcestershire sauce, lemon juice, salt, pepper, garlic powder, and cinnamon. Pour the sauce over the ribs.

3 Cover the pot and cook on low heat for 8 hours.

Makes 4 ½-pound servings

One serving—Calories: 592; Total fat: 23 g; Saturated fat: 9.2 g; Cholesterol: 138 mg; Sodium: 463 mg; Carbohydrates: 47.8 g; Fiber: 0.4 g; Sugar: 46.8 g; Protein: 47.1 g

Diabetic Adjustment: In place of the ¾ cup maple syrup, use ¼ cup maple syrup, ½ cup water, and ½ cup brown sugar substitute. Use unsweetened applesauce. Omit the Worcestershire sauce and garlic powder.

One serving—Calories: 506; Total fat: 23 g; Saturated fat: 9.2 g; Cholesterol: 138 mg; Sodium: 407 mg; Carbohydrates: 19.9 g; Fiber: 0.5 g; Sugar: 16.2 g; Protein: 47 g

Soda Pop Pork Chops

¼ teaspoon salt

¼ teaspoon black pepper

¼ teaspoon garlic powder

⅛ teaspoon red pepper flakes

1 cup gluten-free ketchup

2 tablespoons gluten-free Worcestershire sauce

1 tablespoon light-brown sugar

1 cup cola beverage

4 6-ounce pork chops

1 In a bowl, whisk together the salt, black pepper, garlic powder, red pepper flakes, ketchup, Worcestershire sauce, brown sugar, and cola.

2 Transfer this marinade to a quart-size, reclosable plastic bag.

3 Add the pork chops to the bag. Seal the bag, then push the chops around a little so that all the chops are covered with marinade. Put the pork chops in the refrigerator, and let them marinate for 2 hours.

4 Preheat oven to 350°F. Spray a 9-inch square baking dish with gluten-free nonstick spray. Place the chops in the baking dish. (They will overlap slightly.) Pour any remaining marinade over the chops.

5 Bake for 30 minutes. With the help of an adult, turn over the pork chops with a fork. Continue to bake for another 30 minutes.

Makes 4 pork chops

One pork chop—Calories: 371; Total fat: 17.5 g; Saturated fat: 6.2 g; Cholesterol: 91mg; Sodium: 1,043 mg; Carbohydrates: 25.1 g; Fiber: 0.7 g; Sugar: 24.1 g; Protein: 29 g

Diabetic Adjustment: Omit the garlic powder and Worcestershire sauce. In place of the 1 cup ketchup, use ¼ cup ketchup and ¾ cup salt-free tomato sauce. Use brown sugar substitute in place of the brown sugar. Use sugar-free cola.

One pork chop—Calories: 306; Total fat: 17.2 g; Saturated fat: 6.2 g; Cholesterol: 91 mg; Sodium: 404 mg; Carbohydrates: 7 g; Fiber: 1 g; Sugar: 5.5 g; Protein: 29.2 g

Buffalo Wings

10 chicken wings

1 egg

⅓ cup olive oil

2 tablespoons apple cider vinegar

2 tablespoons gluten-free soy sauce

½ teaspoon salt

¼ teaspoon black pepper

⅛ teaspoon red pepper flakes

¼ teaspoon garlic powder

¼ cup gluten-free ketchup

2 tablespoons brown sugar

1. Preheat oven to 400°F.
2. With the help of an adult, cut off the tip of each chicken wing and throw it away. Cut each chicken wing at the joint to make two small pieces from each wing.
3. In a large bowl, use a whisk to beat the egg and olive oil together.
4. Add the vinegar, soy sauce, salt, black pepper, red pepper flakes, garlic powder, ketchup, and brown sugar. Whisk again until blended.
5. Add the chicken to the bowl. Stir until all the wing pieces are coated with the egg mixture.
6. Spray a baking sheet with gluten-free nonstick spray. Place the wings on the baking sheet.
7. Bake for 35 minutes or until the meat is cooked through. Have an adult help you remove the hot pan from the oven.

Makes 4 5-piece servings

One serving—Calories: 360; Total fat: 29.8 g; Saturated fat: 5.9 g; Cholesterol: 109 mg; Sodium: 542 mg; Carbohydrates: 8.5 g; Fiber: 0.2 g; Sugar: 7.6 g; Protein: 15 g

Chicken and Potatoes

4 boneless, skinless chicken breast halves

5 cloves garlic

4 potatoes

1 lemon

½ cup olive oil

¾ cup water

¼ teaspoon salt

¼ teaspoon pepper

¼ teaspoon mint flakes

1½ teaspoons oregano

1 Preheat oven to 350°F.

2 Place the chicken in an 8″ × 12″ baking dish.

3 Peel the skin off the garlic cloves. Cut the cloves in half lengthwise. Scatter the cut cloves around the chicken.

4 Cut the potatoes in half lengthwise. Cut each half lengthwise into 4 pieces. Place the potatoes around the chicken.

5 Cut the lemon in half. With a fork, squeeze the juice from the lemon into a small bowl. Remove any seeds from the bowl. Sprinkle the lemon juice over the chicken and potatoes.

6 Drizzle the olive oil over the potatoes and chicken.

7 Add the water until you have added enough to almost cover the potatoes.

8 Sprinkle the potatoes and chicken with the salt, pepper, mint flakes, and oregano.

9 Bake the chicken for 30 minutes. Have an adult help you baste the chicken with the pan juices. (If all of the pan juices evaporate, add ¾ cup very hot water to the pan.)

⑩ Continue to bake another 30 minutes until the potatoes and chicken are very tender.

Makes 4 servings (1 chicken breast plus 1 potato)

One serving—Calories: 536; Total fat: 31 g; Saturated fat: 4.7 g; Cholesterol: 96 mg; Sodium: 242 mg; Carbohydrates: 32.2 g; Fiber: 0.7 g; Sugar: 5.2 g; Protein: 38.2 g

Oven-Fried Chicken

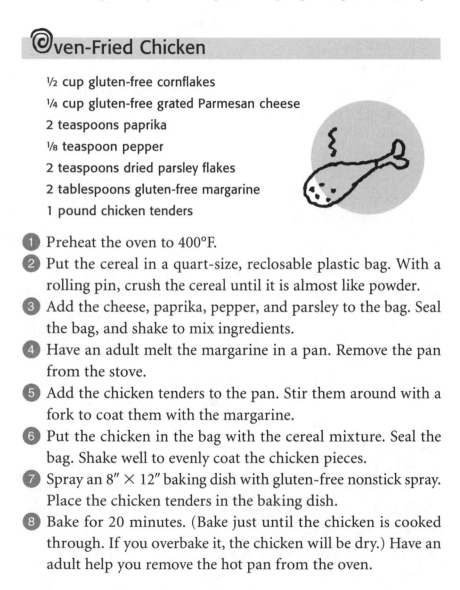

½ cup gluten-free cornflakes

¼ cup gluten-free grated Parmesan cheese

2 teaspoons paprika

⅛ teaspoon pepper

2 teaspoons dried parsley flakes

2 tablespoons gluten-free margarine

1 pound chicken tenders

① Preheat the oven to 400°F.

② Put the cereal in a quart-size, reclosable plastic bag. With a rolling pin, crush the cereal until it is almost like powder.

③ Add the cheese, paprika, pepper, and parsley to the bag. Seal the bag, and shake to mix ingredients.

④ Have an adult melt the margarine in a pan. Remove the pan from the stove.

⑤ Add the chicken tenders to the pan. Stir them around with a fork to coat them with the margarine.

⑥ Put the chicken in the bag with the cereal mixture. Seal the bag. Shake well to evenly coat the chicken pieces.

⑦ Spray an 8″ × 12″ baking dish with gluten-free nonstick spray. Place the chicken tenders in the baking dish.

⑧ Bake for 20 minutes. (Bake just until the chicken is cooked through. If you overbake it, the chicken will be dry.) Have an adult help you remove the hot pan from the oven.

Makes 4 ¼-pound servings

One serving—Calories: 269; Total fat: 11.5 g; Saturated fat: 4.2 g; Cholesterol: 106 mg; Sodium: 255 mg; Carbohydrates: 1.5 g; Fiber: 0.2 g; Protein: 37.3 g

Cheesy Chicken

6 boneless, skinless chicken breast halves

4 tablespoons lemon juice, at room temperature

1½ tablespoons gluten-free margarine, melted

¾ cup crushed gluten-free cornflakes (place cornflakes in a plastic bag, then roll with a rolling pin)

½ teaspoon xanthan gum

½ teaspoon oregano

½ teaspoon salt

½ teaspoon basil

¼ teaspoon garlic powder

⅛ teaspoon cayenne

¼ teaspoon ground thyme

1 tablespoon dried parsley flakes

1 tablespoon butter

6 1-ounce slices provolone cheese

1 Preheat oven to 425°F.

2 Put the chicken breasts between two pieces of waxed paper. Use a meat pounder or your fist to pound the breasts flat.

3 In a shallow bowl, whisk together the lemon juice and melted margarine.

4 Place the cereal crumbs, xanthan gum, oregano, salt, basil, garlic powder, cayenne, thyme, and parsley in a quart-size, reclosable plastic bag. Shake the bag to mix the ingredients.

5 Dip the chicken breasts into the lemon juice mixture, then place them in the bag. Seal the bag, then shake well to coat the chicken evenly with the crumb mixture.

6 Spray an 8″ × 12″ baking pan with gluten-free nonstick spray. Place the chicken pieces in the pan. With dry hands, pat the remaining coating onto the top of the chicken pieces.

7 Cut the butter into tiny pieces. Place the butter pieces on top of the chicken. Lay a piece of cheese on top of each piece of chicken.

8 Bake for 20 minutes or until the chicken is cooked through and is tender when pierced with a fork.

Makes 6 ½–chicken breast servings

One serving—Calories: 413; Total fat: 18.5 g; Saturated fat: 8.6 g; Cholesterol: 133 mg; Sodium: 380 mg; Carbohydrates: 14.2 g; Fiber: 0.5 g; Sugar: 1.5 g; Protein: 45.4 g

Chicken Kabobs

3 wooden skewers
7 ounces boneless, skinless chicken breast
¼ cup gluten-free Italian dressing
2 tablespoons gluten-free soy sauce
⅛ teaspoon black pepper
½ green pepper
1 small onion
8 pineapple chunks

1 Soak the skewers in water for 30 minutes. (This keeps them from burning on the grill.)

2 Wash the chicken. Cut it into ¾-inch squares. Put the chicken in a quart-size, reclosable plastic bag.

3 Add the dressing, soy sauce, and black pepper to the bag. Seal the bag. Gently push the chicken pieces around so the dressing distributes evenly. Refrigerate chicken for at least 1 hour.

4 Cut out the white membrane and seeds from inside the green pepper. Cut the pepper into 4 pieces. Peel the onion, then cut it into 4 wedges.

⑤ Thread the skewers with chicken, green pepper, pineapple, and onion, dividing the ingredients evenly. Throw away any leftover marinade.

⑥ Have an adult preheat the grill, then spray it with a gluten-free nonstick spray. Have an adult help you grill the kabobs for about 10 minutes, turning frequently. Use tongs to turn the chicken. (If it is winter or you don't have a grill, the kabobs may be broiled.)

In place of the chicken, you can use lean pork or ham cubes or raw shrimp.

Makes 4 kabobs

One kabob—Calories: 250; Total fat: 13 g; Saturated fat: 2.5 g; Cholesterol: 48 mg; Sodium: 949 mg; Carbohydrates: 14.5; Fiber: 0.7 g; Sugar: 11 g; Protein: 19 g

Diabetic Adjustment: Use gluten-free, fat-free Italian dressing. Use gluten-free low-salt soy sauce. Use fresh pineapple or canned pineapple packed in juice.

One kabob—Calories: 153; Total fat: 2 g; Saturated fat: 0.5 g; Cholesterol: 48 mg; Sodium: 493 mg; Carbohydrates: 14.5 g; Fiber: 0.7 g; Sugar: 10.5 g; Protein: 19 g

Super-Easy Chicken

1 tablespoon light-brown sugar

¾ cup gluten-free salsa

2 tablespoons gluten-free ketchup

4 5-ounce boneless, skinless chicken breast halves

① In a small bowl, stir together the brown sugar, salsa, and ketchup.

② Spray an 8″ × 12″ baking pan with gluten-free nonstick spray. Lay the chicken pieces in the pan.

③ Spoon the salsa mixture over the chicken pieces.

④ Let the chicken marinate at room temperature for 20 minutes. While it is marinating, preheat the oven to 400°F.

⑤ Bake the chicken for 40 minutes or until it is cooked through. Have an adult help you remove the hot pan from the oven.

Makes 4 ½–chicken breast servings

One serving—Calories: 217; Total fat: 4 g; Saturated fat: 1 g; Cholesterol: 96 mg; Sodium: 518 mg; Carbohydrates: 6.8 g; Fiber: 0 g; Sugar: 5.1 g; Protein: 35.2 g

Diabetic Adjustment: Use brown sugar substitute in place of the brown sugar. Use only 1 tablespoon of gluten-free ketchup.

One serving—Calories: 206; Total fat: 4 g; Saturated fat: 1 g; Cholesterol: 96 mg; Sodium: 474 mg; Carbohydrates: 4 g; Fiber: 0 g; Sugar: 2.5 g; Protein: 35.2 g

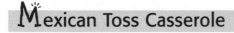

Mexican Toss Casserole

2 15-ounce cans corn kernels (undrained)

2 cups cooked rice

3 5-ounce boneless, skinless chicken breast halves

1 16-ounce can black beans

1 16-ounce jar gluten-free mild chunky salsa

½ cup water

1 cup shredded gluten-free cheddar cheese

① Toss the corn into the bottom of a slow cooker.

② Toss the rice on top of the corn.

3 Cut the chicken breasts into 1-inch cubes. Toss the chicken cubes on top of the rice.

4 Rinse the beans in a strainer under cold running water, then drain. Toss the beans over the chicken.

5 Toss in the salsa and the water.

6 Stir the ingredients to mix.

7 Cook on low power for 7 hours.

8 Just before serving, toss in the cheese. Stir until the cheese has melted.

Makes 6 2-cup servings

One serving—Calories: 375; Total fat: 9.8 g; Saturated fat: 4.5 g; Cholesterol: 67 mg; Sodium: 1,448 mg; Carbohydrates: 41 g; Fiber: 4 g; Sugar: 8.3 g; Protein: 28 g

One-Pot Chicken

4 medium potatoes, cut into wedges

1 cup gluten-free Italian dressing

½ teaspoon basil

1 teaspoon oregano

½ teaspoon garlic powder

1 tablespoon dried parsley flakes

½ cup grated gluten-free Parmesan cheese

3 5-ounce boneless, skinless chicken breast halves, cut into thin strips

¼ cup water

1 Place the potato wedges in the bottom of a slow cooker.

2 Sprinkle the potatoes with ½ cup Italian dressing, ¼ teaspoon basil, ½ teaspoon oregano, ¼ teaspoon garlic powder, 1½ teaspoons parsley, and ¼ cup Parmesan cheese.

3 Put the chicken on top of the potatoes.

4 Pour the water over the chicken. Sprinkle with the remaining ½ cup Italian dressing, ¼ teaspoon basil, ½ teaspoon oregano,

¼ teaspoon garlic powder, 1½ teaspoons parsley, and ¼ cup Parmesan cheese.

5 Cook on low power for 6 hours or until the chicken and potatoes are very tender.

Makes 4 1¾-cup servings

One serving—Calories: 562; Total fat: 37.5 g; Saturated fat: 8.2 g; Cholesterol: 60 mg; Sodium: 1,573 mg; Carbohydrates: 30.7 g; Fiber: 0.5 g; Sugar: 8.2 g; Protein: 25 g

Diabetic Adjustment: Use only 2 medium potatoes. Use gluten-free, fat-free Italian dressing. Omit the cheese.

One serving—Calories: 181; Total fat: 2.2 g; Saturated fat: 0.7 g; Cholesterol: 54 mg; Sodium: 63 mg; Carbohydrates: 18.1 g; Fiber: 0.1 g; Sugar: 5.6 g; Protein: 20.8 g

Milk-Free Adjustment: Use gluten-free, milk-free Italian dressing. Omit the cheese.

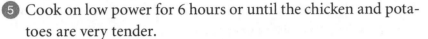 Slow-Cooker Hot Dogs

> 1 package gluten-free hot dogs (10 hot dogs)
> ½ pound gluten-free bacon
> 4 tablespoons brown sugar
> 3 tablespoons gluten-free ketchup

1 Cut the hot dogs in half crosswise to make two shorter hot dogs. Cut each slice of bacon in half.

2 Wrap a strip of bacon around each mini hot dog; secure the bacon with a toothpick at each end of the hot dog.

3 Place one-third of the hot dogs in a slow cooker. Sprinkle with 1 tablespoon plus 1 teaspoon of brown sugar. Drizzle with 1 tablespoon of ketchup. Repeat these layers two more times.

4 Cover the pot. Cook on low heat for 4 hours.

Makes 5 2–hot dog servings

One serving—Calories: 271; Total fat: 22.2 g; Saturated fat: 8.2 g; Cholesterol: 38 mg; Sodium: 818 mg; Carbohydrates: 9.8 g; Fiber: 0 g; Sugar: 6.8 g; Protein: 10 g

Lunch Meat Rolls

1 tablespoon gluten-free cheese spread or cream cheese

1-ounce slice gluten-free lunch meat (turkey breast, roast beef, or ham)

1 teaspoon diced gluten-free pickles

1. Spread cheese on each slice of lunch meat. Sprinkle pickles on top of cheese.

2. Roll up lunch meat into a long cylinder.

Makes 1 serving

One serving (with turkey)—Calories: 145; Total fat: 11 g; Saturated fat: 6.2 g; Cholesterol: 51 mg; Sodium: 283 mg; Carbohydrates: 1.5 g; Fiber: 0 g; Sugar: 1 g; Protein: 10.5 g

Hot Dog Burrito

1 egg

3 teaspoons milk

Dash pepper

1 gluten-free hot dog

1 teaspoon butter

1 slice gluten-free American cheese

1 gluten-free corn tortilla

1 teaspoon gluten-free ketchup

1. In a bowl, whisk together the egg, milk, and pepper.

2. Thinly slice the hot dog.

3. With an adult's help, melt the butter in a skillet.

4. Add the hot dog slices to the skillet. Cook, stirring often, for 1 minute.

⑤ Add the egg mixture to the pan. Cook, stirring constantly, until the egg is cooked.

⑥ Place the cheese on top of the tortilla.

⑦ Spread the ketchup on top of the cheese. Spoon on the egg and hot dog mixture.

⑧ Roll your "sandwich" up like a burrito.

Makes 1 burrito

One burrito—Calories: 466; Total fat: 34.5 g; Saturated fat: 11.3 g; Cholesterol: 263 mg; Sodium: 1,048 mg; Carbohydrates: 22.1 g; Fiber: 1 g; Sugar: 2.1 g; Protein: 18.5 g

Diabetic Adjustment: Use skim milk instead of whole milk. Use a gluten-free, fat-free hot dog. Use gluten-free, fat-free cheese. Omit the ketchup.

One burrito—Calories: 374; Total fat: 17 g; Saturated fat: 3 g; Cholesterol: 237 mg; Sodium: 988 mg; Carbohydrates: 20.8 g; Fiber: 1 g; Sugar: 0.7 g; Protein: 17.5 g

6

Side Dishes

Cold Side Dishes

Egg Bug

1 egg
1 cup shredded lettuce
1 cherry tomato
Gluten-free mayonnaise
1 pitted black olive
1 mini carrot

1. Put the egg in a small pan. Pour in enough water to cover the egg. Put the pan on the stove, and bring the water to a boil. Once the water boils, reduce heat to simmer and let the egg cook for 10 minutes.
2. Have an adult help you remove the hot pan from the stove and pour out the boiling water. Set the pan in the sink, and let cold running water fill the pan. (This helps stop the egg from cooking more.) Remove the egg from the pan.

③ Peel the egg under cold running water. Cut a thin slice from one side of the egg (so it will lie flat without rolling over). Lay the lettuce on a dish. Place the egg on top of the lettuce.

④ Cut the tomato in half. Put a dab of mayonnaise on the cut side of one of the tomato halves, and stick that side to the pointed end of the egg (for the head of your bug). Cut the other tomato half into 4 thin slices. Use a dab of mayonnaise to stick the slices onto the back of your bug (on top of the egg).

⑤ Cut 2 slices from the olive. Use mayonnaise to stick these olive "eyes" to the tomato head. With a toothpick, use mayonnaise to draw a mouth on the tomato "head." Shred the carrot. Use mayonnaise to stick the carrot "hair" to the top of the tomato "head."

Makes 1 Egg Bug

One Egg Bug—Calories: 101; Total fat: 2 g; Saturated fat: 1 g; Cholesterol: 212 mg; Sodium: 126 mg; Carbohydrates: 2.7 g; Fiber: 1 g; Sugar: 0.7 g; Protein: 8 g

Cole Slaw

¾ cup gluten-free mayonnaise

2 tablespoons apple cider vinegar

1 tablespoon sugar

½ teaspoon garlic powder

½ teaspoon salt

½ teaspoon pepper

½ teaspoon paprika

1 8-ounce bag shredded cabbage with shredded carrots

1 small onion, shredded

① In a large bowl, stir together the mayonnaise, vinegar, sugar, garlic powder, salt, pepper, and paprika until smooth. Add the cabbage mix and onion. Stir until blended.

2 Cover with plastic wrap. Refrigerate for several hours to blend flavors.

Makes 6 ¾-cup servings

One serving—Calories: 217; Total fat: 22 g; Saturated fat: 4 g; Cholesterol: 10 mg; Sodium: 361 mg; Carbohydrates: 3 g; Fiber: 1 g; Sugar: 1 g; Protein: 0.5 g

Mixed Bean Salad

1 16-ounce can garbanzo beans

1 16-ounce can black beans

1 16-ounce can kidney beans

1 16-ounce can Great Northern beans

½ green pepper

1 onion

⅓ cup olive oil

3 tablespoons gluten-free balsamic vinegar

¼ teaspoon salt

¼ teaspoon black pepper

¼ teaspoon garlic powder

1 teaspoon dried dill weed

¼ teaspoon mint flakes

¼ teaspoon ground oregano

1 Put all of the beans in a large colander. Rinse well under cold running water, then drain. Transfer the beans to a large bowl. Cut the green pepper and onion into small pieces, and add them to the bowl.

2 In a small bowl, whisk together the olive oil, vinegar, salt, black pepper, garlic powder, dill, mint, and oregano. Pour the dressing over the bean mixture. Stir well to evenly coat the beans. Cover and refrigerate several hours to let the flavors blend.

Makes 10 ¾-cup servings

One serving—Calories: 158; Total fat: 7.6 g; Saturated fat: 0.9 g; Cholesterol: 0 mg; Sodium: 477 mg; Carbohydrates: 19.7 g; Fiber: 5 g; Sugar: 0.9 g; Protein: 6.6 g

Italian Marinated Salad

1 medium cucumber

2 tomatoes

¼ pound gluten-free mozzarella cheese

16 slices gluten-free pepperoni

¼ red onion

¼ teaspoon basil

¼ teaspoon garlic powder

⅛ teaspoon black pepper

¼ teaspoon sugar

⅛ teaspoon red pepper flakes

3 tablespoons gluten-free balsamic vinegar

3 tablespoons olive oil

1. Slice the cucumber, tomatoes, and cheese into ¼-inch-thick slices.
2. Slice the onion very thin.
3. Lay cucumber, tomato, cheese, pepperoni, and onion slices, slightly overlapping, in a circle on each of four salad plates.
4. In a small bowl, stir together the basil, garlic powder, black pepper, sugar, red pepper flakes, vinegar, and olive oil.

Drizzle the dressing over the salads. Cover bowl with plastic wrap and refrigerate for at least 30 minutes before serving to allow flavors to blend.

Makes 4 ¾-cup servings

One serving—Calories: 260; Total fat: 23 g; Saturated fat: 3.5 g; Cholesterol: 16 mg; Sodium: 548 mg; Carbohydrates: 5.6 g; Fiber: 1 g; Sugar: 1.5 g; Protein: 9 g

Milk-Free Adjustment: Omit the cheese and use milk-free pepperoni.

Strawberry Spinach Salad

1 8-ounce bag spinach
1 cup fresh strawberries
½ cup pecans in small pieces
¼ cup shelled sunflower seeds
¼ cup olive oil
1 tablespoon gluten-free balsamic vinegar
2 tablespoons raspberry jam
¼ teaspoon pepper

1. Tear the spinach into large pieces. Divide equally onto six salad plates.
2. Wash the strawberries, then pat dry. Slice each strawberry in half. Divide the strawberry halves evenly among the salad plates. Sprinkle each salad with pecans and sunflower seeds.
3. In a small bowl, whisk together the olive oil, vinegar, jam, and pepper. Drizzle the salad dressing over the salads.

Makes 6 1-cup servings

One serving—Calories: 170; Total fat: 14.8 g; Saturated fat: 1.8 g; Cholesterol: 0 mg; Sodium: 21 mg; Carbohydrates: 9 g; Fiber: 2.3 g; Sugar: 4 g; Protein: 2.5 g

Chicken Salad

¼ small onion

1 rib celery

¼ green pepper

1 tablespoon chopped fresh parsley

1 cup cooked chicken breast

⅔ cup halved seedless grapes

⅛ teaspoon salt

⅛ teaspoon black pepper

¼ cup gluten-free mayonnaise

1 Carefully chop the onion, celery, and green pepper into tiny pieces. Place them in a large bowl. Add the parsley. Cut the chicken into tiny cubes, and add them to the bowl. Add the grapes, salt, black pepper, and mayonnaise. Stir well until combined.

2 Cover the bowl with a piece of plastic wrap. Chill the salad in the refrigerator for an hour to let the flavors blend.

Makes 2 1-cup servings

One serving—Calories: 328; Total fat: 22 g; Saturated fat: 4 g; Cholesterol: 57 mg; Sodium: 193 mg; Carbohydrates: 3.8 g; Fiber: 1.5 g; Sugar: 0.5 g; Protein: 19 g

Cranberry Mold

1 3-ounce box gluten-free strawberry gelatin

1¼ cups boiling water

1 16-ounce can whole-berry cranberry sauce

½ cup finely chopped peeled apple

½ cup finely chopped celery

1 Pour the gelatin into a medium bowl. Have an adult help you add the boiling water. Stir until the gelatin is completely dissolved. In a small bowl, break up the cranberry sauce with a

fork, then add it to the gelatin mixture. Stir until the cranberry sauce is dissolved. Refrigerate the gelatin mixture until it is almost gelled, about 1½ hours.

2 Fold in the apples and celery. Pour the mixture into a mold pan (or keep it in the mixing bowl). Chill until the gelatin is set, about 3 hours.

Makes 4 1-cup servings

One serving—Calories: 302; Total fat: 0.2 g; Saturated fat: 0 g; Cholesterol: 0 mg; Sodium: 125 mg; Carbohydrates: 76 g; Fiber: 2 g; Sugar: 59 g; Protein: 3 g

No-Cook Applesauce

3 apples, any variety
2 tablespoons freshly squeezed
    lemon juice
3 teaspoons sugar
¼ teaspoon cinnamon

1 Peel and core the apples, removing all seeds. Chop the apples into small pieces. Put the apple pieces into a blender. Add the lemon juice. With an adult's help, blend the apples until the mixture is smooth, stopping the machine to scrape down the sides frequently.

2 Pour the applesauce into a bowl, then stir in the sugar and cinnamon.

Makes 4 ¾-cup servings

One serving—Calories: 85; Total fat: 0.5 g; Saturated fat: 0 g; Cholesterol: 0 mg; Sodium: 0 mg; Carbohydrates: 22 g; Fiber: 2.7 g; Sugar: 19 g; Protein: 0.2 g

Diabetic Adjustment: Use brown sugar substitute in place of the sugar.

One serving—Calories: 63; Total fat: 0.5 g; Saturated fat: 0 g; Cholesterol: 0 mg; Sodium: 0 mg; Carbohydrates: 14.5 g; Fiber: 2.7 g; Sugar: 12 g; Protein: 0.2 g

Cranberry Cherry Mold

1 16-ounce can jellied cranberry sauce

1 16½-ounce can pitted dark sweet cherries

1 10½-ounce can crushed pineapple

1 6-ounce box gluten-free cherry gelatin

1 cup chopped walnuts

1 Melt the cranberry sauce in a medium saucepan over low heat.

2 Drain the juice from the cherries into a 2-cup measuring cup.

3 Cut the cherries into quarters. Stir them into the melted cranberry sauce.

4 Stir in the pineapple, including the juice from the can.

5 Remove the pan from the heat.

6 Add enough water to the reserved cherry juice to make 2 cups. Pour the juice and water into a small saucepan.

7 Put the gelatin into a medium bowl.

8 Bring the cherry juice mixture to a boil on the stove.

9 Have an adult help you pour the boiling cherry mixture over the gelatin. Stir until the gelatin is completely dissolved.

10 Stir in the cranberry mixture.

11 Stir the nuts into the gelatin mixture.

12 Pour the gelatin mixture into a mold or a 9″ × 13″ baking pan. Refrigerate until firm, about 5 hours.

Makes 18 3- by 2-inch servings

One serving—Calories: 136; Total fat: 2 g; Saturated fat: 0.2 g; Cholesterol: 0 mg; Sodium: 36 mg; Carbohydrates: 28.6 g; Fiber: 0.7 g; Sugar: 23 g; Protein: 2 g

Diabetic Adjustment: Use fruits packed in juice. Use gluten-free, sugar-free gelatin. Omit the walnuts.

One serving—Calories: 53; Total fat: 0 g; Saturated fat: 0 g; Cholesterol: 0 mg; Sodium: 32 mg; Carbohydrates: 12.9 g; Fiber: 0.3 g; Sugar: 10 g; Protein: 1.2 g

Hot Side Dishes

Mexican Rice

1 small onion
3 tablespoons butter
1 cup long-grain rice
2 tablespoons canned chopped
    green chilies
1 cup very hot water
1 gluten-free chicken bouillon cube
1 cup gluten-free salsa

1 Peel and chop the onion.

2 Melt the butter in a medium saucepan over medium heat. Have an adult help you sauté the onion and rice in the butter, stirring frequently, until the rice is golden.

3 Add the chilies, hot water, bouillon cube, and salsa, stirring until blended. Cover the pan, and lower the heat. Let the rice steam for 15 to 20 minutes until all the liquid is absorbed.

Makes 4 ¾-cup servings

One serving—Calories: 203; Total fat: 9.5 g; Saturated fat: 0 g; Cholesterol: 23 mg; Sodium: 726 mg; Carbohydrates: 26 g; Fiber: 0.7 g; Sugar: 2.2 g; Protein: 2.5 g

Spinach and Rice

2 10-ounce boxes frozen chopped spinach, thawed
¾ cup rice
½ cup tomato sauce
1¾ cups water
3 tablespoons olive oil
1 tablespoon dill weed

¼ teaspoon salt

¼ teaspoon pepper

1 tablespoon dried minced onion

1. Preheat oven to 350°F.

2. Squeeze the spinach dry. Put it in a medium bowl.

3. Add the rice to the bowl, and stir with a fork, breaking up the spinach.

4. Put the tomato sauce, water, olive oil, dill, salt, pepper, and minced onion in a small saucepan. Put the pan on the stove, and bring it to a boil over high heat.

5. Have an adult help you remove the pan and pour the sauce over the spinach and rice.

6. Stir to blend well.

7. Spray an 8-inch square pan with gluten-free nonstick spray. Spoon the spinach mixture into the pan.

8. Bake for 30 minutes or until the rice is tender and most of the liquid has been absorbed. Have an adult help you remove the hot pan from the oven.

Makes 6 2½- by 4-inch servings

One serving—Calories: 130; Total fat: 7 g; Saturated fat: 0.8 g; Cholesterol: 0 mg; Sodium: 232 mg; Carbohydrates: 14.6 g; Fiber: 1.6 g; Sugar: 0.6 g; Protein: 3.2 g

Diabetic Adjustment: Reduce rice to ½ cup. Use salt-free tomato sauce. Reduce olive oil to 2 tablespoons.

One serving—Calories: 74; Total fat: 2.5 g; Saturated fat: 0.3 g; Cholesterol: 0 mg; Sodium: 144 mg; Carbohydrates: 11 g; Fiber: 1.6 g; Sugar: 0.6 g; Protein: 2.8 g

Polka-Dot Rice

2¼ cups water

2 gluten-free beef bouillon cubes

⅛ teaspoon pepper

1 tablespoon dried parsley flakes

⅓ cup frozen peas

1 cup rice

 Put the water, bouillon cubes, pepper, and parsley in a medium saucepan. Bring to a boil on the stove.

2 When the water is boiling, have an adult help you stir in the peas and rice. Lower heat to simmer, and cover pan with a lid. Simmer about 15 minutes or until all the water is absorbed.

Makes 4 ½-cup servings

One serving—Calories: 77; Total fat: 1 g; Saturated fat: 1 g; Cholesterol: 0 mg; Sodium: 658 mg; Carbohydrates: 16 g; Fiber: 1 g; Sugar: 2.7 g; Protein: 3 g

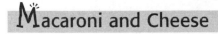
Macaroni and Cheese

½ pound (8 ounces) gluten-free corn elbow macaroni

2 eggs

3½ cups milk

2½ cups grated gluten-free sharp cheddar cheese

¼ teaspoon salt

¼ teaspoon pepper

¼ cup gluten-free margarine, cut in small pieces

1. Have an adult help you cook the macaroni in boiling water according to package directions. Drain the macaroni in a colander.
2. Whisk the eggs and milk together in a large bowl. Add the pasta, and stir to blend. Add the cheese, salt, pepper, and margarine. Stir well to blend. Spray a slow cooker with gluten-free nonstick spray. Spoon the pasta mixture into the slow cooker. Cook for 4½ hours on low power.

Makes 4 1½-cup servings

One serving—Calories: 536; Total fat: 28.5 g; Saturated fat: 13.3 g; Cholesterol: 166 mg; Sodium: 602 mg; Carbohydrates: 11.2 g; Fiber: 6.7 g; Sugar: 10.5 g; Protein: 20.9 g

Breaded Veggies

1 cup broccoli florets, cut into bite-size pieces

1 cup whole, fresh button mushrooms

1 cup cauliflower florets, cut into bite-size pieces

3 cups gluten-free cornflake crumbs

¼ teaspoon salt

Dash pepper

½ teaspoon oregano

⅛ teaspoon basil

¼ teaspoon garlic powder

¼ teaspoon paprika

3 tablespoons grated gluten-free Romano cheese

2 tablespoons gluten-free Italian dressing

⅓ cup gluten-free mayonnaise

1 Preheat oven to 425°F.

2 Wash the broccoli, mushrooms, and cauliflower florets. Pat them dry with a paper towel.

3 Put the cereal in a quart-size, reclosable plastic bag. Add the salt, pepper, oregano, basil, garlic powder, paprika, and cheese to the cereal bag. Seal the bag, and shake well to mix ingredients.

4 In another quart-size, reclosable plastic bag, place the Italian dressing and mayonnaise. Seal the bag well. Press the contents to blend. Add the vegetable pieces. Reseal the bag, then shake the bag to evenly coat the vegetables.

5 Transfer the vegetables to the cereal bag. Seal the bag, then shake it well to evenly coat the vegetables with the cereal crumb mixture.

6 Spray a baking sheet with gluten-free nonstick spray. Place the veggies on the baking sheet. Bake for 10 minutes or until lightly browned. Have an adult help you remove the hot baking sheet from the oven.

Makes 4 ¾-cup servings

One serving—Calories: 237; Total fat: 18 g; Saturated fat: 3.7 g; Cholesterol: 9.5 mg; Sodium: 590 mg; Carbohydrates: 16 g; Fiber: 3.7 g; Sugar: 10.5 g; Protein: 5 g

Corn Casserole

1 16-ounce can gluten-free cream-style corn

2 tablespoons sugar

¼ teaspoon salt

⅔ cup milk

2 tablespoons butter, melted

¼ cup Gluten-Free Flour Mixture (See the Hints chapter.)

2 eggs

½ cup gluten-free corn chips

¼ teaspoon paprika

1. Preheat oven to 325°F.
2. In a bowl, stir together the corn, sugar, salt, milk, and melted butter until blended.
3. Sprinkle the flour mixture in gradually, stirring until blended.
4. In a small bowl, beat the eggs with a fork, then stir them into the corn mixture.
5. Butter a 1-quart casserole dish. Pour the corn mixture into the dish.
6. Put the corn chips into a sandwich-size, self-seal reclosable plastic bag. Seal the bag securely, then crush the chips.
7. Add the paprika to the bag. Reseal and shake the bag until the paprika and chips are mixed.
8. Sprinkle the crushed corn chips on top of the casserole.
9. Bake until set (about 30 minutes). Have an adult help you remove the hot casserole from the oven.

Makes 4 ¾-cup servings

One serving—Calories: 242; Total fat: 11 g; Saturated fat: 1.5 g; Cholesterol: 126 mg; Sodium: 563 mg; Carbohydrates: 31.5 g; Fiber: 1.5 g; Sugar: 12.7 g; Protein: 7 g

Diabetic Adjustment: Omit sugar and salt. Use 1% milk in place of whole milk. Use gluten-free, salt-free margarine in place of the butter.

One serving—Calories: 206; Total fat: 8.3 g; Saturated fat: 2 g; Cholesterol: 107 mg; Sodium: 428 mg; Carbohydrates: 17 g; Fiber: 1.5 g; Sugar: 8.9 g; Protein: 6.4 g

Potato and Broccoli Casserole

1 8-ounce package frozen chopped broccoli

¾ cup water

3 tablespoons butter

⅛ teaspoon garlic powder

⅛ teaspoon salt

⅛ teaspoon pepper

1½ cups gluten-free instant mashed potato flakes

½ cup milk

½ cup shredded gluten-free cheddar cheese

1 egg, slightly beaten

Paprika

1. Preheat oven to 325°F.

2. Have an adult help you steam the broccoli according to the package directions, then drain completely and squeeze dry.

3. Put the water, butter, garlic powder, salt, and pepper in a medium saucepan. Put the pan on the stove, and bring the water to a boil. Have an adult remove the pan from the stove and place it on a pot holder.

4. Using a fork, stir the potato flakes, milk, cheese, and egg into the water until well blended. (Be careful not to burn yourself on the hot pan.) Then stir in the broccoli.

5. Spray a 2-quart casserole with gluten-free nonstick spray. Spoon the potato mixture into the casserole. Sprinkle the top lightly with paprika.

6. Bake, uncovered, for 20 minutes. Have an adult help you remove the hot casserole from the oven.

Makes 4 1-cup servings

One serving—Calories: 263; Total fat: 16 g; Saturated fat: 4.2 g; Cholesterol: 94 mg; Sodium: 328 mg; Carbohydrates: 18.5 g; Fiber: 0.3 g; Sugar: 1.5 g; Protein: 4.2 g

Hash Brown Casserole

1 16-ounce package gluten-free frozen hash brown potatoes,
    thawed

3 tablespoons canned chopped green chilies

¼ teaspoon salt

¼ teaspoon pepper

1 tablespoon dried
    parsley flakes

1 14½-ounce can gluten-free stewed tomatoes

4 ounces gluten-free processed cheese, diced

1 Spray a 2-quart microwave-safe casserole with gluten-free nonstick spray. Place the potatoes in the casserole.

2 Stir in the green chilies, salt, pepper, parsley, and tomatoes (including the juice).

3 Cover the casserole. Microwave the casserole on High for 6 minutes.

4 Stir the ingredients. Return the casserole to the microwave for 8 more minutes on High.

5 With the help of an adult, remove the casserole to a counter. Stir in the cheese. (The pan may be very hot.)

6 Microwave the casserole on High for 2 minutes. Stir, then cook for 2 more minutes.

This casserole may be baked in the oven instead of the microwave. Before you prepare the casserole, preheat the oven to 400°F. Bake for 40 minutes, stirring in the cheese after 20 minutes.

Makes 6 ¾-cup servings

One serving—Calories: 198; Total fat: 4.3 g; Saturated fat: 2.8 g; Cholesterol: 17 mg; Sodium: 495 mg; Carbohydrates: 33.5 g; Fiber: 1.5 g; Sugar: 5 g; Protein: 6.5 g

Creamy Potatoes

1 16-ounce bag gluten-free frozen shredded hash brown potatoes, thawed

½ teaspoon salt

½ teaspoon celery salt

½ teaspoon garlic powder

1 tablespoon dried onion flakes

1 tablespoon dried parsley flakes

1 cup whipping cream

½ cup whole milk

1 cup shredded gluten-free sharp cheddar cheese

1 cup gluten-free cornflake crumbs

4 tablespoons butter

Paprika

1. Preheat oven to 350°F.
2. In a large bowl, stir together the potatoes, salt, celery salt, garlic powder, onion flakes, parsley, whipping cream, milk, and cheese.
3. Spray a 9″ × 13″ baking pan with gluten-free nonstick spray. Spoon the potato mixture into the pan.
4. Sprinkle the cornflake crumbs on top of the potatoes.
5. Have an adult help you melt the butter. Drizzle the butter evenly over the crumbs.
6. Sprinkle paprika on top.
7. Bake for 55 minutes or until the potatoes are tender.
8. Have an adult help you take the hot pan out of the oven.

Makes 12 ½-cup servings

One serving—Calories: 187; Total fat: 12.8 g; Saturated fat: 6.2 g; Cholesterol: 41 mg; Sodium: 224 mg; Carbohydrates: 11.8 g; Fiber: 0.4 g; Sugar: 3.3 g; Protein: 3.7 g

Potato Buffet

This is a fun side dish that allows everyone to top his or her potatoes as desired.

> 2 large baking potatoes
> Corn oil
> Toppings (selected from "Topping Suggestions")

Topping Suggestions

> Gluten-free sour cream or plain gluten-free low-fat yogurt
> Chopped chives or green onions
> Gluten-free bacon bits (Have an adult help you cook the bacon.)
> Grated gluten-free Parmesan cheese
> Broccoli in cheese sauce (Have an adult help you steam frozen chopped broccoli, then drain it well. Put it in a glass bowl, and sprinkle it with gluten-free shredded cheese. Put it in the microwave until melted.)
> Chili (Most supermarkets sell gluten-free canned chili, or you may make your own.)

1. Preheat oven to 400°F.
2. Wash each potato. Cut each potato in half lengthwise. Brush the outside of each half with a little bit of corn oil.
3. Put one pair of potato halves together (cut sides facing each other). Wrap the potato in foil. Repeat this procedure with the other two halves.
4. Bake the potatoes for 1¼ hours or until tender throughout.
5. While the potatoes bake, set out bowls with the different toppings.
6. Have an adult help you remove the potatoes from the oven and unwrap the foil. Set one-half of a potato on each person's plate. Let each person put on the desired toppings.

Makes 4 ½-potato servings

One serving (no toppings)—Calories: 93; Total fat: 0 g; Saturated fat: 0 g; Cholesterol: 0 mg; Sodium: 7 mg; Carbohydrates: 22.2 g; Fiber: 0.5 g; Sugar: 2.2 g; Protein: 2 g

Roasted Potatoes

16 small red-skinned potatoes

2 tablespoons olive oil

½ teaspoon salt

¼ teaspoon pepper

¾ teaspoon dill weed

1 tablespoon grated gluten-free Parmesan cheese

1 Preheat oven to 350°F.

2 Cut the potatoes into ½-inch cubes; put them in a large bowl. Drizzle the olive oil over the potatoes. Stir with a spoon to mix well. Spray a 9″ × 13″ baking pan with gluten-free non-stick spray. Transfer the potatoes to the baking pan. Sprinkle the salt, pepper, dill, and cheese over the top.

3 Cover the pan with foil. Bake the potatoes for 40 minutes or until tender. Have an adult help you remove the hot pan from the oven.

Makes 4 1-cup servings

One serving—Calories: 195; Total fat: 7.5 g; Saturated fat: 1.5 g; Cholesterol: 2 mg; Sodium: 351 mg; Carbohydrates: 28.7 g; Fiber: 0.7 g; Sugar: 3 g; Protein: 3.7 g

Cheesy Tomatoes

¼ cup gluten-free cornflake crumbs

3 tablespoons grated gluten-free Parmesan cheese

¼ teaspoon garlic powder

¼ teaspoon oregano

⅛ teaspoon pepper

4 tomatoes

2 tablespoons gluten-free Italian dressing

1. Preheat oven to 400°F.
2. In a small bowl, stir together the cornflake crumbs, cheese, garlic powder, oregano, and pepper.
3. Cut the top fourth off each tomato.
4. Set the tomatoes, cut side up, in an 8-inch square pan.
5. Drizzle the Italian dressing on top of each tomato.
6. Sprinkle each tomato with the crumb mixture.
7. Bake for 10 minutes or until the crumb mixture is toasted.
8. Have an adult help you remove the hot pan from the oven.

Makes 4 tomatoes

One tomato—Calories: 119; Total fat: 7.2 g; Saturated fat: 1.7 g; Cholesterol: 3 mg; Sodium: 355 mg; Carbohydrates: 11.7 g; Fiber: 2 g; Sugar: 2.2 g; Protein: 3 g

Diabetic Adjustment: Omit the cheese. Use gluten-free, fat-free dressing.

One tomato—Calories: 48; Total fat: 0.5 g; Saturated fat: 0 g; Cholesterol: 0 mg; Sodium: 286 mg; Carbohydrates: 11.2 g; Fiber: 2 g; Sugar: 1.8 g; Protein: 1.5 g

Spinach with Cheese

3 10-ounce boxes frozen chopped spinach, thawed

1½ cups grated gluten-free Swiss cheese

¼ teaspoon pepper

¼ teaspoon salt

½ teaspoon dill weed

2 tablespoons olive oil

1. Preheat oven to 350°F.
2. Squeeze most of the moisture out of the spinach. Put the spinach in a medium bowl.
3. Stir in the cheese, pepper, salt, dill, and olive oil.
4. Spray a 9-inch square pan with gluten-free nonstick spray. Spoon the spinach mixture into the pan.
5. Bake for 20 minutes. (Do not overbake, or it will dry out.) Have an adult help you remove the hot pan from the oven.

Makes 9 3-inch-square servings

One serving—Calories: 110; Total fat: 8.2 g; Saturated fat: 3.7 g; Cholesterol: 17 mg; Sodium: 156 mg; Carbohydrates: 2.8 g; Fiber: 1.3 g; Sugar: 0 g; Protein: 7 g

Glazed Yams

1 1-pound, 13-ounce can yams packed in syrup

¼ teaspoon salt

¼ teaspoon pepper

¼ teaspoon cinnamon

Dash ground cloves

¼ cup corn syrup

½ cup chopped pecans

½ cup brown sugar

¾ cup crushed gluten-free cornflakes

5 tablespoons butter

1 Preheat oven to 350°F.

2 Drain the yams in a sieve over a bowl, reserving ½ cup of the syrup. Spray an 8″ × 12″ baking pan with gluten-free non-stick spray. Place the yams in the baking pan.

3 In a medium bowl, stir together the reserved ½ cup of syrup from the yams and the salt, pepper, cinnamon, cloves, and corn syrup. Drizzle this sauce over the yams. Sprinkle the yams with pecans.

4 In a medium bowl, stir together the brown sugar and crushed cornflakes. Have an adult help you melt the butter in a small saucepan. Pour the butter over the cornflake mixture. Using a fork, mix well to distribute the butter evenly. Sprinkle this mixture over the yams.

5 Bake for 25 minutes. Have an adult help you take the hot pan out of the oven.

Makes 6 ¾-cup servings

One serving—Calories: 248; Total fat: 11.3 g; Saturated fat: 0.4 g; Cholesterol: 25 mg; Sodium: 253 mg; Carbohydrates: 57.5 g; Fiber: 3.9 g; Sugar: 35.3 g; Protein: 0.8 g

Diabetic Adjustment: In place of the corn syrup, use ¼ cup brown sugar substitute mixed with ¼ cup additional yam syrup. In place of the brown sugar, use brown sugar substitute. In place of the butter, use gluten-free, low-fat margarine.

One serving—Calories: 214; Total fat: 8 g; Saturated fat: 0.8 g; Cholesterol: 0 mg; Sodium: 160 mg; Carbohydrates: 37 g; Fiber: 3.9 g; Sugar: 18.8 g; Protein: 1 g

Orange Beets

3 tablespoons butter

6 tablespoons orange juice

2 tablespoons brown sugar

2 15½-ounce cans sliced beets

1 Melt the butter in a medium saucepan over medium heat. Add the orange juice and brown sugar, stirring until the sugar has dissolved.

2 Drain the beets in a sieve. Add them to the sauce in the pan. Stir to coat the beets evenly with sauce. Heat until beets are hot.

Makes 6 ½-cup servings

One serving—Calories: 87; Total fat: 6 g; Saturated fat: 2.2 g; Cholesterol: 15 mg; Sodium: 93 mg; Carbohydrates: 8.1 g; Fiber: 0.8 g; Sugar: 7.3 g; Protein: 0.7 g

Diabetic Adjustment: Use gluten-free, low-fat margarine in place of the butter. Use brown sugar substitute in place of the brown sugar.

One serving—Calories: 64; Total fat: 4.5 g; Saturated fat: 1 g; Cholesterol: 0 mg; Sodium: 105 mg; Carbohydrates: 5.6 g; Fiber 0.8 g; Sugar: 4.8 g; Protein: 0.7 g

Milk-Free Adjustment: Use gluten-free, milk-free margarine in place of the butter.

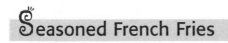

Seasoned French Fries

4 medium russet potatoes
1 ½ tablespoons olive oil
¼ teaspoon salt
⅛ teaspoon pepper
¼ teaspoon garlic powder
2 teaspoons oregano

1 Preheat oven to 400°F.

2 Slice the potatoes lengthwise into thin strips. (Younger children many need an adult's help with this.)

3 Put olive oil in a large bowl. Stir in the salt, pepper, garlic powder, and oregano.

4 Add the potatoes. Toss the potatoes with a spoon to coat them evenly.

5 Spoon the potatoes onto a cookie sheet. Make sure they are in a single layer, not overlapping each other.

6 Bake for 30 minutes or until potatoes are golden brown. Have an adult help you remove the hot pan from the oven.

Makes 4 24-fry servings

One serving—Calories: 169; Total fat: 5.2 g; Saturated fat: 0.7 g; Cholesterol: 0 mg; Sodium: 157 mg; Carbohydrates: 28.5 g; Fiber: 0.7 g; Sugar: 3 g; Protein: 2.5 g

Potatoes and Mushrooms

2 tablespoons plus 3 tablespoons olive oil

3 large russet potatoes

½ teaspoon salt

½ teaspoon minced garlic (from a jar)

½ teaspoon basil

1 8-ounce can sliced mushrooms

1 Preheat oven to 350°F.

2 Pour 2 tablespoons of olive oil in the bottom of a 9-inch square baking dish. Tilt the dish to distribute the oil evenly.

3 Thinly slice the potatoes.

4 Lay the potatoes on the bottom of the baking dish.

5 Sprinkle the potatoes with half of the salt, garlic, and basil.

6 Drain the mushrooms. Layer them on top of the potatoes and seasonings.

7 Drizzle the remaining 3 tablespoons of olive oil over the mushrooms.

8 Sprinkle the remaining salt, garlic, and basil over the mushrooms.

9 Bake for 45 minutes or until the potatoes are tender. Have an adult help you remove the hot pan from the oven.

Makes 4 4½-inch-square servings

One serving—Calories: 257; Total fat: 17 g; Saturated fat: 2.5 g; Cholesterol: 0 mg; Sodium: 304 mg; Carbohydrates: 24.7 g; Fiber: 1 g; Sugar: 4.7 g; Protein: 2.7 g

Dilled Peas

1 10-ounce box frozen peas

1 ½ tablespoons butter

½ teaspoon dill weed

⅛ teaspoon salt

1 teaspoon lemon juice

1. Put the peas in a 1-quart saucepan, and barely cover them with water.
2. Put the pan on the stove. Over high heat, bring the water to a boil.
3. Cover the pan, and reduce the heat to simmer. Let the peas simmer slowly for 3 minutes.
4. With the help of an adult, remove the pan from the stove, and put the peas in a strainer to drain.
5. Put the peas back into the pan (but not back on the stove).
6. Add the butter, dill, salt, and lemon juice. Stir until the butter has melted.

Makes 3 3⅓-ounce servings

One serving—Calories: 106; Total fat: 5.6 g; Saturated fat: 0 g; Cholesterol: 13 mg; Sodium: 338 mg; Carbohydrates: 10.8 g; Fiber: 3 g; Sugar: 6 g; Protein: 4 g

Diabetic Adjustment: Use gluten-free, low-fat margarine in place of the butter.

One serving—Calories: 94; Total fat: 4 g; Saturated fat: 0.7 g; Cholesterol: 0 mg; Sodium: 348 mg; Carbohydrates: 10.8 g; Fiber: 3 g; Sugar: 6 g; Protein: 4 g

Milk-Free Adjustment: Use gluten-free, milk-free margarine in place of the butter.

Tomato Potatoes

4 medium russet potatoes

1 large tomato

2 green onions

¼ cup olive oil

½ teaspoon salt

¼ teaspoon pepper

1 tablespoon oregano

¼ teaspoon garlic powder

¾ cup crumbled gluten-free feta cheese

1 cup water

1 Preheat oven to 350°F.

2 Chop the potatoes and tomatoes into 1-inch cubes.

3 Thinly slice the green onions.

4 Put the potatoes, tomatoes, green onions, olive oil, salt, pepper, oregano, garlic powder, cheese, and water into a medium bowl. Stir with a spoon to coat the vegetables evenly.

5 Spray an 8″ × 12″ baking pan with gluten-free nonstick spray. Put the potato mixture into the pan.

6 Bake for 1 hour or until the potatoes are tender. Have an adult help you take the hot pan out of the oven.

Makes 5 1-cup servings

One serving—Calories: 274; Total fat: 17 g; Saturated fat: 5.8 g; Cholesterol: 25 mg; Sodium: 561 mg; Carbohydrates: 25 g; Fiber: 0.8 g; Sugar: 2.4 g; Protein: 6.2 g

7

Desserts

Paintbrush Cookies

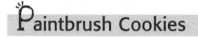

Gluten-free cookie dough (prepared by an adult)

3 egg yolks

3 tablespoons water

3 different food colorings

Colored gluten-free sprinkles (optional)

1. Make one recipe of your favorite sugar cookie dough.
2. Roll out cookie dough, ½" thick. Cut with cookie cutters, then place cookies on a baking sheet.
3. Place an egg yolk in each of three small cups. Add 1 tablespoon of water to each cup. Using a fork, mix the water and egg yolk in each cup.
4. Add a drop of food coloring to each cup; blend with a spoon.
5. With a clean paintbrush, use the colored egg yolks to "paint" the top of the cookies, making beautiful designs and pictures. If you like, add colored gluten-free sprinkles.

6 Have an adult help you bake your creations following the cookie recipe directions.

Makes 1 ½-cup serving of "paint"

Rocky Road Bars

½ cup butter

½ cup white sugar

½ cup brown sugar

½ cup gluten-free peanut butter

1 teaspoon vanilla

1 teaspoon gluten-free mayonnaise

2 eggs

1½ cups Gluten-Free Flour Mixture (See the Hints chapter.)

1 cup semisweet chocolate chips

2 cups gluten-free miniature marshmallows

1 cup chopped unsalted peanuts

1 Preheat oven to 375°F.

2 Have an adult melt the butter.

3 In a large bowl, stir together the melted butter, white and brown sugars, peanut butter, vanilla, mayonnaise, and eggs.

4 Sift the flour mixture over the egg mixture. Stir until well blended.

5 Spray a 9″ × 13″ pan with gluten-free nonstick spray. Press the dough into the pan.

6 Bake for 10 minutes.

7 Have an adult remove the hot pan from the oven. Sprinkle the chocolate chips, marshmallows, and peanuts over the top. Let an adult put the pan back in the oven to bake another 5 to 8 minutes, until marshmallows puff and get lightly browned. Cool and cut into 3″ × 2″ bars.

Makes 18 3- by 2-inch bars

One bar—Calories: 240; Total fat: 14 g; Saturated fat: 2.9 g; Cholesterol: 30 mg;
Sodium: 114 mg; Carbohydrates: 26.5 g; Fiber: 1 g; Sugar: 16.3 g; Protein: 4.3 g

Diabetic Adjustment: Use gluten-free, low-fat margarine in place of the butter. Omit the mayonnaise. Use brown sugar substitute in place of the white and brown sugars. Use gluten-free, low-fat peanut butter. Use 1 egg plus 2 egg whites in place of the 2 eggs. Omit the marshmallows.

One bar—Calories: 201; Total fat: 12.5 g; Saturated fat: 4.8 g; Cholesterol: 17 mg;
Sodium: 149 mg; Carbohydrates: 19.4 g; Fiber: 1 g; Sugar: 7.6 g; Protein: 4.2 g

Milk-Free Adjustment: Use gluten-free, milk-free margarine in place of the butter. Omit the mayonnaise.

Toffee Squares

1 cup butter, melted

1 cup brown sugar

2 eggs

1 ½ teaspoons vanilla

2 cups Gluten-Free Flour Mixture (See the Hints chapter.)

¾ cup semisweet chocolate chips

½ cup chopped walnuts

1 Preheat oven to 350°F.

2 Put the butter, brown sugar, eggs, and vanilla in a large bowl. Mix with a whisk until smooth.

3 Sift the flour mixture over the bowl. Stir until it is completely blended.

4 Spray a 9″ × 13″ baking pan with gluten-free nonstick spray. Spread the dough on the pan. Bake 15 minutes. Have an adult help you remove the hot pan from the oven.

5 Sprinkle the chocolate chips on top of the dough and bake another 2 minutes. With a knife or metal spatula, spread out the melted chocolate chips to form an even coating on top.

6 Sprinkle the nuts on top of the chocolate. Cool before cutting into 30 bars.

Makes 30 3- by 1⅓-inch bars

One bar—Calories: 138; Total fat: 8.9 g; Saturated fat: 1 g; Cholesterol: 30 mg; Sodium: 72 mg; Carbohydrates: 10 g; Fiber: 0.3 g; Sugar: 6.9 g; Protein: 1.3 g

Diabetic Adjustment: Use gluten-free, low-fat margarine in place of the butter. Use brown sugar substitute in place of the brown sugar. Use 1 egg plus 2 egg whites for the 2 eggs.

One bar—Calories: 106; Total fat: 7 g; Saturated fat: 2.2 g; Cholesterol: 7 mg; Sodium: 86 mg; Carbohydrates: 6 g; Fiber: 0.3 g; Sugar: 0.3 g; Protein: 1.3 g

Milk-Free Adjustment: Use gluten-free, milk-free margarine in place of the butter.

Chocolate Mint Bars

1½ cups Gluten-Free Flour Mixture (See the Hints chapter.)

2 cups sugar

1 teaspoon salt

¾ cup cocoa (unsweetened)

2 teaspoons gluten-free baking powder

5 eggs

⅔ cup gluten-free margarine, melted

3 teaspoons vanilla

3 tablespoons light corn syrup

2 cups chopped nuts

Frosting

¼ cup gluten-free margarine

2 cups confectioners' sugar, sifted

2 tablespoons milk

1 teaspoon mint extract

2 drops green food coloring

1 Preheat oven to 350°F.

2 Sift the flour mixture, sugar, salt, cocoa, and baking powder into a large bowl. Stir in the eggs, margarine, vanilla, and corn syrup. Mix thoroughly. Fold in the nuts.

3 Spray a 9″ × 13″ baking pan with gluten-free nonstick spray. Spoon the batter into the pan. Bake for 40 minutes or until a toothpick inserted near the center comes out clean. (Do not overbake, or the cookies will be dry.) Have an adult remove the hot pan from the oven. Cool the pastry on a wire rack.

4 To make the frosting, melt the margarine in a medium bowl on High in the microwave. Add the confectioners' sugar, milk, mint extract, and food coloring in a bowl. Use a whisk to mix thoroughly. Using a knife, spread the frosting over the cooled pastry. (If the frosting is too thin, add a little more confectioners' sugar. If it is too thick, add a little more milk.)

5 Place the pan in the freezer for 15 minutes to set the frosting. Remove the pan from the freezer, and cut into 40 bars.

Makes 40 2½- by 1⅓-inch bars

One bar—Calories: 253; Total fat: 16.7 g; Saturated fat: 3.6 g; Cholesterol: 34 mg; Sodium: 192 mg; Carbohydrates: 25.8 g; Fiber: 0.9 g; Sugar: 13 g; Protein: 4.2 g

Diabetic Adjustment: Use brown sugar substitute in place of the sugar in the pastry. Use skim milk. Use gluten-free, low-fat margarine. Use 3 whole eggs and 4 egg whites in place of the 5 eggs. Do not frost.

One bar—Calories: 186; Total fat: 13.8 g; Saturated fat: 2.2 g; Cholesterol: 16 mg; Sodium: 139 mg; Carbohydrates: 13.8 g; Fiber: 0.9 g; Sugar: 1.4 g; Protein: 4 g

Milk-Free Adjustment: Use gluten-free, milk-free margarine. Use soy milk in place of the milk.

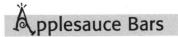pplesauce Bars

½ cup gluten-free margarine

1 cup thick applesauce

3 eggs

1 tablespoon gluten-free mayonnaise

1 cup brown sugar

2¼ cups Gluten-Free Flour Mixture (See the Hints chapter.)

2 teaspoons gluten-free baking powder

1 teaspoon baking soda

½ teaspoon salt

1 teaspoon cinnamon

1 cup raisins

Confectioners' sugar

1. Preheat oven to 350°F.
2. Have an adult melt the margarine.
3. In a large bowl, mix the margarine, applesauce, eggs, and mayonnaise with a whisk. Stir in the brown sugar.
4. Sift the flour mixture, baking powder, baking soda, salt, and cinnamon over the applesauce and egg mixture. With a spoon, stir the dough until blended.
5. Stir in the raisins.
6. Spray a 9″ × 13″ baking pan with gluten-free nonstick spray. Spread the batter in the pan.
7. Bake the cookies for 20 minutes. Have an adult help you remove the hot pan from the oven.
8. When the cookies have cooled, sift confectioners' sugar over the top. Cut into 30 bars.

Makes 30 3- by 1⅓-inch bars

One bar—Calories: 105; Total fat: 3.5 g; Saturated fat: 1.1 g; Cholesterol: 24 mg; Sodium: 80 mg; Carbohydrates: 16.6 g; Fiber: 0.6 g; Sugar: 9.7 g; Protein: 1.7 g

Diabetic Adjustment: Use unsweetened applesauce. Use 2 eggs plus 2 egg whites in place of the 3 eggs. Omit the mayonnaise. Use brown sugar substitute in place of the brown sugar.

One bar—Calories: 84; Total fat: 3 g; Saturated fat: 1 g; Cholesterol: 17 mg; Sodium: 78 mg; Carbohydrates: 12.5 g; Fiber: 0.7 g; Sugar: 5.6 g; Protein: 1.7 g

Milk-Free Adjustment: Use milk-free margarine. Omit the mayonnaise.

Almond Macaroons

¼ cup Gluten-Free Flour Mixture (See the Hints chapter.)

2 cups shredded coconut

1 cup chopped almonds

⅔ cup sweetened condensed milk

½ teaspoon vanilla

1 teaspoon almond extract

1 Sift the flour mixture into a bowl.

2 Stir the coconut and almonds into the flour with a wooden spoon.

3 Stir in the milk, vanilla, and almond flavoring until the ingredients are combined.

4 Spray cookie sheets with gluten-free nonstick spray.

5 Drop the dough by teaspoonfuls onto the cookie sheet. Make sure the cookies are about 2 inches from each other. Refrigerate the cookie sheets for 1 hour before baking. (This will keep the cookies from spreading too much.)

6 Preheat oven to 325°F.

7 Bake for 10 to 12 minutes or until the cookies turn a light brown.

8 Have an adult help remove the hot cookie sheets from the oven. Let the cookies cool on the cookie sheets for 2 minutes to set. Remove them with a spatula to finish cooling on a rack.

For a special occasion, before you mix the batter, put the coconut in a plastic bag. Add a few drops of food coloring. Seal the bag and shake to evenly color the coconut. You could use green for St. Patrick's Day, yellow for Easter, red for the 4th of July, and so on.

Makes 24 cookies

One cookie—Calories: 82; Total fat: 30 g; Saturated fat: 3.4 g; Cholesterol: 2 mg; Sodium: 32 mg; Carbohydrates: 11 g; Fiber: 1.4 g; Sugar: 8.8 g; Protein: 0.7 g

No-Bake Peanut Butter Cookies

½ cup sugar

½ cup light corn syrup

1 cup gluten-free peanut butter

¼ cup chopped peanuts

2½ cups gluten-free cornflakes

1 Put the sugar and corn syrup into a large bowl. Heat in the microwave on High for 1½ minutes. Remove from oven and stir. If the sugar is not completely dissolved, return the bowl to the microwave for 30 seconds. (Do not let the mixture boil, or the sugar will crystallize and harden.)

2 Stir in the peanut butter, and mix well.

3 Stir in the peanuts and cornflakes. Mix until evenly coated.

4 Using a teaspoon dipped in a bowl of cold water, drop the cookie mixture by teaspoonfuls onto waxed paper. Let the cookies set for 30 minutes.

Makes 30 cookies

One cookie—Calories: 101; Total fat: 4.4 g; Saturated fat: 0.5 g; Cholesterol: 0 mg; Sodium: 59 mg; Carbohydrates: 13.5 g; Fiber: 0.7 g; Sugar: 9.4 g; Protein: 2.6 g

Black and White Brownies

4 eggs

⅔ cup corn oil

1 tablespoon gluten-free mayonnaise

2 teaspoons vanilla

2 cups Gluten-Free Flour Mixture (See the Hints chapter.)

½ teaspoon salt

⅓ cup cocoa (unsweetened)

⅔ cup brown sugar

⅔ cup white sugar

½ cup semisweet chocolate chips

½ cup white chocolate chips

¾ cup chopped macadamia nuts

Confectioners' sugar

1. Preheat oven to 350°F.
2. In a large bowl, whisk the eggs until frothy.
3. Whisk in the corn oil, mayonnaise, and vanilla.
4. Sift the flour mixture, salt, cocoa, and brown and white sugars over the eggs. Stir to blend well. Stir in the semisweet and white chocolate chips and the macadamia nuts. Mix until well blended.
5. Spray a 9-inch square pan with gluten-free nonstick spray. Pour the batter into the pan.
6. Bake for 25 minutes or until a toothpick inserted in the center comes out clean.
7. Have an adult help you remove the hot pan from the oven.
8. When the brownies have cooled, sift confectioners' sugar over the top. Cut into 18 bars.

Makes 18 3- by 1½-inch brownies

One brownie—Calories: 408; Total fat: 18 g; Saturated fat: 4.9 g; Cholesterol: 48 mg; Sodium: 205 mg; Carbohydrates: 57.2 g; Fiber: 1.7 g; Sugar: 17 g; Protein: 7.2 g

Diabetic Adjustment: Use 2 whole eggs and 4 egg whites in place of the 4 whole eggs. Use brown sugar substitute in place of the white and brown sugars. Omit the mayonnaise. Omit the white chocolate chips. Omit the confectioners' sugar.

One brownie—Calories: 327; Total fat: 15.6 g; Saturated fat: 3.5 g; Cholesterol: 24 mg; Sodium: 198 mg; Carbohydrates: 43 g; Fiber: 1.7 g; Sugar: 4.2 g; Protein: 6.8 g

Milk-Free Adjustment: Omit the mayonnaise and white chocolate chips.

Orange Jar Bars

3 eggs
½ cup white sugar
½ cup corn oil
½ cup orange juice
1 tablespoon grated orange zest
1 teaspoon vanilla
1 cup Gluten-Free Flour Mixture (See the Hints chapter.)
2½ teaspoons gluten-free baking powder
½ teaspoon salt
Confectioners' sugar

1 Preheat oven to 350°F.
2 Break the eggs into a 1-quart jar with a tight-fitting lid. Cover the jar, and shake it 15 times.
3 Add the sugar, corn oil, orange juice, orange zest, and vanilla. Cover the jar, and shake it 20 more times.

④ Sift the flour mixture, baking powder, and salt onto waxed paper. Carefully lift the waxed paper, and pour the dry ingredients into the jar. Shake 40 more times or until the batter is smooth.

⑤ Spray an 8-inch square pan with gluten-free nonstick spray. Pour the batter into the pan.

⑥ Bake for 20 minutes or until the bars begin to pull away from the sides of the pan. Have an adult help you take the hot pan out of the oven.

⑦ Let the bars cool in the pan. Sift confectioners' sugar over the top. Cut into 16 bars.

Makes 16 2-inch squares

One square—Calories: 122; Total fat: 7.7 g; Saturated fat: 1.1 g; Cholesterol: 40 mg; Sodium: 86 mg; Carbohydrates: 11.2 g; Fiber: 0.2 g; Sugar: 5.6 g; Protein: 2 g

Diabetic Adjustment: Use 2 whole eggs and 2 egg whites in place of the 3 eggs. Use brown sugar substitute in place of the white sugar. Omit the confectioners' sugar.

One square—Calories: 105; Total fat: 7.4 g; Saturated fat: 1 g; Cholesterol: 27 mg; Sodium: 92 mg; Carbohydrates: 7.4 g; Fiber: 0.2 g; Sugar: 2 g; Protein: 2.2 g

Best-Ever Jumbo Chocolate Cookies

1½ cups semisweet chocolate chips

¾ cup brown sugar

¼ cup butter, softened

3 eggs

2 teaspoons vanilla

½ cup Gluten-Free Flour Mixture (See the Hints chapter.)

¾ teaspoon gluten-free baking powder

1 cup chopped walnuts (optional)

1. Preheat oven to 350°F.
2. Put ¾ cup of the chocolate chips into a large microwave-safe bowl. Microwave on High for 40 seconds. Stir the chocolate, then continue to microwave until melted (about another 15 seconds).
3. Stir in the sugar, butter, eggs, and vanilla.
4. Sift the flour mixture and baking powder over the chocolate mixture. Stir in until blended, scraping down the sides of the bowl frequently. Stir in the remaining ¾ cup of chocolate chips and the nuts.
5. Drop the batter by ¼-cupfuls onto an ungreased cookie sheet.
6. Bake 12 minutes or until the cookies are puffed and no imprint is left when you touch the top of a cookie lightly. Have an adult help you remove the hot cookie sheet from the oven. Remove the cookies from the cookie sheet with a spatula. Let the cookies cool on a wire rack.

Makes 18 cookies

One cookie (without walnuts)—Calories: 106; Total fat: 8.8 g; Saturated fat: 3.6 g; Cholesterol: 42 mg; Sodium: 54 mg; Carbohydrates: 19.5 g; Fiber: 0.1 g; Sugar: 14.3 g; Protein: 1.4 g

Diabetic Adjustment: Use only 6 ounces (¾ cup) of chocolate chips, and omit adding more chocolate chips in step 4. Use brown sugar substitute in place of the brown sugar. Use gluten-free, low-fat margarine in place of the butter. Use 2 whole eggs and 2 egg whites in place of the 3 eggs.

One cookie (without walnuts)—Calories: 86; Total fat: 5.1 g; Saturated fat: 2.3; Cholesterol: 24 mg; Sodium: 48 mg; Carbohydrates: 8.5 g; Fiber: 0.1 g; Sugar: 4.7 g; Protein: 1.6 g

Milk-Free Adjustment: Use gluten-free, milk-free margarine in place of the butter.

Coconut Nut Bars

1 cup Gluten-Free Flour Mixture (See the Hints chapter.)

½ cup butter

3 tablespoons white sugar

2 eggs

1 cup chopped walnuts

½ cup shredded coconut

1½ cups brown sugar

Confectioners' sugar (optional)

1 Preheat oven to 350°F.

2 Sift the flour mixture into a medium bowl.

3 With the back of a fork, blend in the butter. Add the white sugar, continuing to blend with the fork until the butter is in teeny pieces.

4 Lightly spray an 8-inch square pan with gluten-free nonstick spray. Pat the pastry into the bottom of the pan.

5 In the same bowl, whisk the eggs until frothy. Stir in the walnuts, coconut, and brown sugar.

6 Spoon the egg mixture over the pastry.

7 Bake for 30 minutes. Have an adult help you take the hot pan out of the oven. Cool the cookies in the pan. Cut into 16 squares. If desired, sift confectioners' sugar over the tops of the cooled bars.

Makes 16 2-inch squares

One square—Calories: 180; Total fat: 11.6 g; Saturated fat: 1.6 g; Cholesterol: 42 mg; Sodium: 78 mg; Carbohydrates: 18.4 g; Fiber: 1 g; Sugar: 11.4 g; Protein: 2.3 g

Diabetic Adjustment: Use gluten-free, low-fat margarine in place of the butter. Use unsweetened coconut. Use brown sugar substitute in place of the brown sugar.

One square—Calories: 122; Total fat: 9.9 g; Saturated fat: 1.6 g; Cholesterol: 33 mg; Sodium: 79 mg; Carbohydrates: 8 g; Fiber: 1 g; Sugar: 0.4 g; Protein: 2.3 g

Milk-Free Adjustment: Use gluten-free, milk-free margarine in place of the butter.

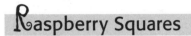aspberry Squares

Crust

1 cup Gluten-Free Flour Mixture (See the Hints chapter.)

2 teaspoons gluten-free baking powder

1 tablespoon sugar

½ cup gluten-free margarine, softened

2 eggs

1 tablespoon milk

Filling

½ cup raspberry jam

1 teaspoon almond extract

Topping

1 egg

4 tablespoons gluten-free margarine, melted

1 teaspoon vanilla

1 cup sugar

2 cups shredded coconut

1 Preheat oven to 350°F.

2 To make the crust, sift the flour mixture and baking powder into a medium bowl. With the back of a fork, work the sugar and margarine into the flour mixture until it is like small crumbs. In a small bowl, whisk the eggs until frothy. Add the eggs and milk to the flour mixture, mixing well until blended.

③ Lightly spray a 9-inch square pan with gluten-free nonstick spray. With lightly floured hands, pat the pastry in the bottom of the pan.

④ To make the filling, stir together the raspberry jam and almond extract in a small bowl. Spread the filling over the pastry.

⑤ To make the topping, whisk together the egg, melted margarine, and vanilla in a medium bowl. Stir the sugar into the egg mixture. Stir in the coconut. With the back of a spoon, spread the topping evenly over the raspberry layer.

⑥ Bake for 30 minutes or until the topping is golden brown. Have an adult help you remove the hot pan from the oven. Cool the pastry in the pan. Cut into 16 squares.

Makes 16 2¼-inch squares

One square—Calories: 264; Total fat: 16.3 g; Saturated fat: 6.4 g; Cholesterol: 44 mg; Sodium: 173 mg; Carbohydrates: 26 g; Fiber: 1.7 g; Sugar: 18.4 g; Protein: 1.9 g

Diabetic Adjustment: Use brown sugar substitute in place of the white sugar. Use gluten-free, low-fat margarine. Use skim milk. Use all-fruit jam. Use unsweetened coconut.

One square—Calories: 172; Total fat: 11.3 g; Saturated fat: 3.8 g; Cholesterol: 40 mg; Sodium: 178 mg; Carbohydrates: 17.3 g; Fiber: 1.7 g; Sugar: 6.2 g; Protein: 1.9 g

Milk-Free Adjustment: Use gluten-free, milk-free margarine. Use soy milk in place of the milk.

Peanut Butter Cookies

1 cup plus ¼ cup granulated sugar

1 cup gluten-free creamy peanut butter

1 egg

1 13-ounce bag gluten-free chocolate stars or kisses

1 Preheat oven to 350°F.

2 In a medium bowl, stir together 1 cup of sugar and the peanut butter and egg. Mix until completely blended.

3 Put a tablespoon of dough into your hands, and roll it into a ball about the size of a walnut. Repeat with the remaining dough.

4 Pour remaining ¼ cup of granulated sugar into a small bowl. Roll the dough balls in the sugar (adding more granulated sugar to bowl if needed), then place them on an ungreased cookie sheet.

5 Press a chocolate star or kiss into the center of each cookie.

6 Bake for 10 to 12 minutes.

7 Have an adult help you remove the hot cookie sheet from the oven. Let the cookies set on the cookie sheet for 3 minutes. Use a spatula to remove them to a wire rack to let them cool.

Makes 40 cookies

One cookie—Calories: 69; Total fat: 4.3 g; Saturated fat: 1.1 g; Cholesterol: 5 mg; Sodium: 26 mg; Carbohydrates: 6.3 g; Fiber: 4 g; Sugar: 5 g; Protein: 1.9 g

Diabetic Adjustment: Use brown sugar substitute in place of the sugar. Use gluten-free, low-sugar peanut butter. Omit rolling the cookies in additional sugar. Use gluten-free, sugar-free candies on the top.

One cookie—Calories: 22; Total fat: 4.3 g; Saturated fat: 1.6 g; Cholesterol: 5 mg; Sodium: 15 mg; Carbohydrates: 3.4 g; Fiber: 0.4 g; Sugar: 2.1 g; Protein: 1.7 g

Mississippi Mud Cake

5 eggs

3 tablespoons milk

2 teaspoons vanilla

2 cups sugar

⅓ cup cocoa (unsweetened)

1 ½ cups Gluten-Free Flour Mixture (See the Hints chapter.)

2 teaspoons gluten-free baking powder

1 cup chopped walnuts

¾ cup mini semisweet chocolate chips

32 ounces gluten-free marshmallow creme

Frosting

½ cup (1 stick) gluten-free margarine

⅓ cup cocoa (unsweetened)

1 box confectioners' sugar

¼ cup evaporated milk

1 teaspoon vanilla

1 Preheat oven to 350°F.

2 In a medium bowl, whisk the eggs, milk, and vanilla until frothy. Sift the sugar, cocoa, flour mixture, and baking powder over the egg mixture. Stir until blended. Stir in the walnuts and chocolate chips.

3 Spray a 9″ × 13″ baking pan with gluten-free nonstick spray. Pour the batter into the pan. Bake the cake for 25 minutes or until a toothpick inserted in the center comes out clean. Have an adult help you remove the hot pan from the oven.

4 While the cake is still hot, spread the marshmallow creme over the top of the cake. Let the cake cool for 10 minutes before icing it.

5 To make the frosting, have an adult help you melt the margarine in a medium saucepan. When melted, remove the pan from the stove.

6 Sift the cocoa and sugar onto a piece of waxed paper. Carefully lift the paper, and pour the cocoa and sugar mixture into the saucepan with the melted margarine. Mix until blended. Stir in the milk and vanilla. Spread the icing over the slightly warm cake. (If the frosting is too thick to spread, add a little more milk.)

Makes 24 3- by 1½-inch servings

One serving—Calories: 297; Total fat: 8 g; Saturated fat: 2.8 g; Cholesterol: 47 mg; Sodium: 151 mg; Carbohydrates: 52.6 g; Fiber: 0.7 g; Sugar: 25.6 g; Protein: 5.5 g

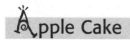

Apple Cake

2 eggs

½ cup corn oil

¼ cup water

¾ teaspoon vanilla

½ teaspoon salt

1 cup Gluten-Free Flour Mixture (See the Hints chapter.)

1 teaspoon baking soda

1 cup sugar

1 teaspoon cinnamon

1 can gluten-free apple pie filling

1 cup chopped walnuts

¼ cup confectioners' sugar

1 Preheat oven to 350°F.

2 Whisk the eggs in a large bowl until very frothy.

3 Whisk in the corn oil, water, and vanilla.

4 Sift the salt, flour mixture, baking soda, sugar, and cinnamon over the egg mixture. Whisk to blend ingredients.

5 Gently stir in the apple pie filling and walnuts.

6 Spray an 8″ × 12″ baking pan with gluten-free nonstick spray. Pour the batter into the pan.

7 Bake for 40 minutes or until a toothpick inserted in the center comes out clean. Have an adult help you remove the hot pan from the oven. Once the cake has cooled, sift confectioners' sugar over top of cake.

Makes 12 4- by 2-inch servings

One serving—Calories: 216; Total fat: 14 g; Saturated fat: 1.8 g; Cholesterol: 35 mg; Sodium: 133 mg; Carbohydrates: 21.5 g; Fiber: 1.2 g; Sugar: 20.7 g; Protein: 3 g

Diabetic Adjustment: Use 1 whole egg and 2 egg whites in place of the 2 eggs. Use brown sugar substitute in place of the brown sugar. Use canned apple slices (drained) in place of the apple pie filling. Omit the confectioners' sugar.

One serving—Calories: 157; Total fat: 11.8 g; Saturated fat: 1.5 g; Cholesterol: 18 mg; Sodium: 108 mg; Carbohydrates: 11.5 g; Fiber: 1.1 g; Sugar: 3.1 g; Protein: 2.3 g

Upside-Down Fruit Salad Cake

¼ cup shredded coconut

1½ cups Gluten-Free Flour Mixture (See the Hints chapter.)

2 teaspoons baking soda

½ teaspoon salt

½ teaspoon cinnamon

¼ teaspoon nutmeg

1 cup sugar

1 cup corn oil

2 eggs

2 teaspoons vanilla

½ cup blueberries, washed and drained

1 large banana, diced

1 8-ounce can crushed pineapple (undrained)

½ cup chopped pecans

1 Preheat oven to 350°F.

2 Put the coconut in a blender. Have an adult help you blend it until it is like a powder. Set aside.

3 Over a medium bowl, sift together the flour mixture, baking soda, salt, cinnamon, and nutmeg.

4 In a large bowl, whisk together the sugar, corn oil, eggs, and vanilla until smooth. With a spoon, stir in the flour mixture, mixing until combined. Gently fold in the blueberries, banana, pineapple, and pecans.

⑤ Spray an 8″ × 12″ baking pan with gluten-free nonstick spray. Sprinkle the powdered coconut evenly across the bottom of the pan. Pour the batter into the pan.

⑥ Bake for 55 minutes or until a toothpick inserted in the center comes out clean.

⑦ Have an adult help you remove the hot pan from the oven.

⑧ Cool the pan on a wire rack for 10 minutes, then have an adult invert the pan onto a plate, then remove the pan. Cool the cake completely.

Makes 12 4- by 2-inch servings

One serving—Calories: 327; Total fat: 23.1 g; Saturated fat: 3.6 g; Cholesterol: 35 mg; Sodium: 116 mg; Carbohydrates: 28 g; Fiber: 1.9 g; Sugar: 13.5 g; Protein: 3.1 g

Diabetic Adjustment: Use unsweetened coconut. Use brown sugar substitute in place of the sugar. Use 1 whole egg and 2 egg whites in place of the 2 eggs. Use pineapple packed in juice.

One serving—Calories: 270; Total fat: 21.3 g; Saturated fat: 3 g: Cholesterol: 18 mg; Sodium: 116 mg; Carbohydrates: 17.4 g; Fiber: 1.9 g; Sugar: 3.3 g; Protein: 3 g

Fruity Coconut Cake

3 eggs

½ teaspoon vanilla

1 15-ounce can fruit cocktail, undrained

¼ cup applesauce

½ cup shredded coconut

1 cup white sugar

½ cup brown sugar

2 cups Gluten-Free Flour Mixture (See the Hints chapter.)

2 teaspoons baking soda

¼ teaspoon salt

1 8-ounce container gluten-free nondairy whipped topping, thawed

1. Preheat oven to 325°F.
2. With a whisk, whip eggs and vanilla in a bowl until very frothy.
3. Stir in the fruit cocktail (including the syrup in the can), applesauce, and coconut.
4. Sift the white and brown sugars, flour mixture, baking soda, and salt over the egg mixture.
5. Stir the batter until blended.
6. Spray a 9″ × 13″ pan with gluten-free nonstick spray. Pour the batter into the pan.
7. Bake for 30 to 35 minutes or until a toothpick inserted in the center comes out clean.
8. Have an adult place the hot cake pan on a rack to cool.
9. When the cake has cooled, spread the top with the whipped topping.

Makes 24 3- by 1½-inch servings

One serving—Calories: 135; Total fat: 3.7 g; Saturated fat: 3.3 g; Cholesterol: 27 mg; Sodium: 45 mg; Carbohydrates: 22.4 g; Fiber: 1.1 g; Sugar: 12.8 g; Protein: 1.9 g

Diabetic Adjustment: Use fruit packed in juice. Use unsweetened applesauce and unsweetened coconut. Use brown sugar substitute for the brown sugar. Omit the whipped topping.

One serving—Calories: 53; Total fat: 1.8 g; Saturated fat: 1.3 g; Cholesterol: 27 mg; Sodium: 43 mg; Carbohydrates: 11.9 g; Fiber: 1.1 g; Sugar: 2.4 g; Protein: 1.8 g

Milk-Free Adjustment: Omit the whipped topping.

Chocolate Pudding Cake

This cake will have the pudding on the bottom with the cake on top.

1 cup Gluten-Free Flour Mixture (See the Hints chapter.)

2 tablespoons cocoa (unsweetened)

3 teaspoons gluten-free baking powder

¼ teaspoon salt

½ cup brown sugar

½ cup milk

1½ tablespoons corn oil

2 teaspoons vanilla

Topping

½ cup brown sugar

3 tablespoons cocoa (unsweetened)

1¾ cups boiling water

1 Preheat oven to 350°F.

2 Sift the flour mixture, cocoa, baking powder, and salt over a large bowl. Stir in the brown sugar. Stir in the milk, corn oil, and vanilla until smooth. Spread the batter evenly in a greased 9-inch square baking pan.

3 To make the topping, stir together the brown sugar and cocoa in a small bowl. Sprinkle the topping over the batter.

4 Have an adult pour the boiling water evenly over the topping.

5 Bake for 35 minutes. Have an adult help you test whether the cake is done by tapping the top lightly. If your finger doesn't leave an imprint, the cake is done. Remove from oven and cool.

Makes 9 3-inch-square servings

One serving—Calories: 191; Total fat: 3.7 g; Saturated fat: 1.2 g; Cholesterol: 4 mg; Sodium: 159 mg; Carbohydrates: 36.8 g; Fiber: 0.6 g; Sugar: 14.6 g; Protein: 4 g

Diabetic Adjustment: Use brown sugar substitute in place of the brown sugar. Use skim milk in place of whole milk.

One serving—Calories: 131; Total fat: 2.8 g; Saturated fat: 0.6 g; Cholesterol: 1 mg; Sodium: 159 mg; Carbohydrates: 23.6 g; Fiber: 0.6 g; Sugar: 1.7 g; Protein: 4 g

Milk-Free Adjustment: Use soy milk in place of the milk.

Chocolate Peanut Butter Pie

Crust

  1 cup gluten-free peanut butter

  1 cup corn syrup

  4 cups gluten-free puffed-rice cereal

Filling

  1 pint gluten-free chocolate ice cream, partially softened

  ¾ cup gluten-free peanut butter

Frosting

  4 tablespoons gluten-free margarine

  ⅓ cup cocoa (unsweetened)

  ½ teaspoon vanilla

  1½ cups sifted confectioners' sugar

  2 tablespoons milk

  2 tablespoons chopped peanuts

1 To make the crust, use a rubber spatula to blend the peanut butter and corn syrup in a medium bowl. Add the cereal, and mix well. Press into a 9-inch pie plate.

2 To make the filling, spoon the ice cream into a bowl. With a whisk, fold in the peanut butter so it is streaked through the ice cream. Spoon the filling into the pie crust.

3 To make the frosting, have an adult help you melt the marga-rine in a pan. Remove the pan from the stove. Stir in the cocoa

and vanilla. Alternately add the confectioners' sugar and the milk, beating with a whisk until the frosting is just thin enough to spread. (Add a teeny bit more milk if needed.) Using a knife, spread the frosting on the pie. Sprinkle peanuts on top of the frosting.

4 Cover the pie with foil. Freeze until firm, about 4 hours.

Makes 8 servings

One serving—Calories: 760; Total fat: 38.6 g; Saturated fat: 8.5 g; Cholesterol: 19 mg; Sodium: 145 mg; Carbohydrates: 92.1 g; Fiber: 3.7 g; Sugar: 54.8 g; Protein: 19.8 g

Cheesecake Pie

1 cup gluten-free small-curd cottage cheese

1 8-ounce package gluten-free cream cheese, softened

2 eggs

½ cup sugar

3 tablespoons fresh lemon juice

½ teaspoon almond extract

½ teaspoon vanilla

1 Preheat oven to 350°F.

2 Place the cottage cheese, cream cheese, eggs, sugar, lemon juice, almond extract, and vanilla in a blender.

③ With the help of an adult, cover the blender and blend for 20 seconds. Scrape down the sides, then cover and blend again for 20 seconds.

④ Spray a 9-inch pie plate with gluten-free nonstick spray. Pour the mixture into the pie plate.

⑤ Bake for 25 minutes or until a knife inserted in the center comes out clean.

⑥ Have an adult help you remove the hot pie from the oven. Set it on a wire rack to cool. Once the pie is completely cool, refrigerate it for several hours before serving.

For a special touch, serve topped with raspberries, strawberries, or blueberries.

Makes 8 servings

One serving—Calories: 105; Total fat: 5 g; Saturated fat: 2.8 g; Cholesterol: 68 mg; Sodium: 126 mg; Carbohydrates: 9.3 g; Fiber: 0 g; Sugar: 8.2 g; Protein: 5.3 g

Diabetic Adjustment: Use gluten-free, low-fat cottage cheese and cream cheese. Use brown sugar substitute in place of the sugar.

One serving—Calories: 50; Total fat: 1.5 g; Saturated fat: 0.5 g; Cholesterol: 54 mg; Sodium: 156 mg; Carbohydrates: 2.1 g; Fiber: 0 g; Sugar: 1.2 g; Protein: 6.8 g

Chocolate Chip Pie

1 cup (2 sticks) gluten-free margarine

3 eggs

1 teaspoon vanilla

½ cup Gluten-Free Flour Mixture (See the Hints chapter.)

2 teaspoons gluten-free baking powder

½ cup white sugar

½ cup brown sugar

¾ cup semisweet chocolate chips

1 cup chopped walnuts

1. Preheat oven to 325°F.
2. Have an adult help you melt the margarine in a pan. Remove the pan from the heat and let it cool.
3. In a large bowl, whip the eggs and vanilla with a whisk until foamy.
4. Sift the flour mixture and baking powder over the eggs. Add the white and brown sugars. Whisk until the ingredients are well blended. Add the cooled margarine, and stir until blended. Stir in the chocolate chips and walnuts.
5. Spray a 10-inch pie plate with gluten-free nonstick spray. Pour the batter into the pie plate.
6. Bake for 50 minutes or until a toothpick inserted in the center comes out clean.
7. Have an adult remove the hot pie from the oven. Let cool on a wire rack.

Makes 8 servings

One serving—Calories: 503; Total fat: 38.5 g; Saturated fat: 13.2 g; Cholesterol: 104 mg; Sodium: 295 mg; Carbohydrates: 36.1 g; Fiber: 0.7 g; Sugar: 25.6 g; Protein: 4.6 g

Diabetic Adjustment: Use gluten-free, low-fat margarine. Use 2 eggs and 4 egg whites in place of the 3 eggs. Use brown sugar substitute in place of the brown sugar. Use only ½ cup walnuts.

One serving—Calories: 332; Total fat: 26.7 g; Saturated fat: 8.5 g; Cholesterol: 53 mg; Sodium: 318 mg; Carbohydrates: 19.8 g; Fiber: 0.3 g; Sugar: 10.8 g; Protein: 3.7 g

Milk-Free Adjustment: Be sure chocolate chips are semisweet chocolate (not milk chocolate).

Apple Cranberry Cobbler

1 21-ounce can gluten-free apple pie filling

1 16-ounce can whole cranberry sauce

¼ cup Gluten-Free Flour Mixture (See the Hints chapter.)

½ teaspoon cinnamon

¼ cup brown sugar

½ cup chopped nuts

⅓ cup (5⅓ tablespoons) gluten-free margarine

1 Preheat oven to 400°F.

2 Cut the apples into small chunks. (This will be a messy job!)

3 In a 9-inch square baking pan, stir together the pie filling and cranberry sauce.

4 Over a small bowl, sift together the flour mixture and cinnamon. Stir in the brown sugar till blended. Stir the nuts into the sugar mixture.

5 Sprinkle the sugar mixture evenly over the top of the fruit.

6 Put margarine in a glass measuring cup. Heat it in the microwave on High for 50 seconds or until the margarine is melted.

7 Drizzle the melted margarine over the top of the dessert.

8 Bake for 25 minutes or until the whole dessert is bubbling. May be served warm or at room temperature.

Makes 9 ⅔-cup servings

One serving—Calories: 215; Total fat: 10.6 g; Saturated fat: 2.6 g; Cholesterol: 7 mg; Sodium: 100 mg; Carbohydrates: 30 g; Fiber: 1.1 g; Sugar: 22.2 g; Protein: 1.4 g

Diabetic Adjustment: Use gluten-free, low-fat margarine. Use brown sugar substitute in place of the brown sugar.

One serving—Calories: 185; Total fat: 8.7 g; Saturated fat: 1.5 g; Cholesterol: 0 mg; Sodium: 104 mg; Carbohydrates: 26.7 g; Fiber: 1.1 g; Sugar: 19 g; Protein: 1.4 g

Peach Bread Pudding

3 eggs

½ cup brown sugar

¼ teaspoon salt

1¼ cups milk

1 teaspoon vanilla

½ teaspoon nutmeg

¾ teaspoon cinnamon

2 cups gluten-free bread cubes

⅔ cup diced canned peaches, drained

1. Preheat oven to 350°F.
2. In a large bowl, whip the eggs with a whisk until frothy.
3. Add the brown sugar, salt, milk, vanilla, nutmeg, and cinnamon. Whisk until the ingredients are blended.
4. Stir in the bread cubes and peaches.
5. Spray an 8-inch square baking pan with gluten-free nonstick spray. Pour the pudding into the pan. Let the pan set on the counter for 20 minutes so the bread may absorb some of the liquid.
6. Bake for 40 minutes. Have an adult help you remove the hot pan from the oven. Best when served warm.

In place of the peaches, you can use blueberries or raisins.

Makes 9 2⅔-inch-square servings

One serving—Calories: 105; Total fat: 2.6 g; Saturated fat: 1.1 g; Cholesterol: 52 mg; Sodium: 148 mg; Carbohydrates: 17 g; Fiber: 0.9 g; Sugar: 12.3 g; Protein: 3.6 g

Diabetic Adjustment: Use 1 egg and 4 egg whites in place of the 3 eggs. Use brown sugar substitute in place of the brown sugar. Use 1% milk in place of whole milk. Use juice-packed peaches.

One serving—Calories: 67; Total fat: 1.3 g; Saturated fat: 0.5 g; Cholesterol: 25 mg; Sodium: 153 mg; Carbohydrates: 10.3 g; Fiber: 0.9 g; Sugar: 5.8 g; Protein: 3.6 g

Milk-Free Adjustment: Use soy milk in place of the milk.

Pumpkin Streusel Pudding

1 15-ounce can pumpkin

1 14-ounce can sweetened condensed milk

1 egg

1 teaspoon cinnamon

½ teaspoon nutmeg

½ teaspoon ground cloves

½ teaspoon ginger

½ teaspoon salt

Topping

¼ cup brown sugar

¼ teaspoon cinnamon

2 tablespoons Gluten-Free Flour Mixture (See the Hints chapter.)

2 tablespoons cold butter

¾ cup walnuts, chopped

1. Preheat oven to 425°F.
2. In a large bowl, whisk together the pumpkin, condensed milk, egg, cinnamon, nutmeg, cloves, ginger, and salt.
3. Spray a 9-inch pie plate with gluten-free nonstick spray. Pour the pudding into the pie plate.
4. Bake for 15 minutes. Have an adult help you remove the hot pudding from the oven.
5. While the pudding is baking, make the topping. In a small bowl, mix the brown sugar and cinnamon. Use a fork to stir the flour mixture into the cinnamon and sugar.

6 Blend in the butter until the mixture is crumbly. Stir in the walnuts.

7 Sprinkle the topping over the pudding.

8 Reduce the oven temperature to 350°F. Bake the pudding for 40 minutes or until a knife inserted near the center comes out clean.

9 Cool the pudding completely, then refrigerate for 3 or more hours.

Makes 9 3-inch-square servings

One serving—Calories: 262; Total fat: 10.5 g; Saturated fat: 2.7 g; Cholesterol: 41 mg; Sodium: 212 mg; Carbohydrates: 38 g; Fiber: 39.1 g; Sugar: 33.6 g; Protein: 5.5 g

Cherry Whip Pudding

1 10-ounce can crushed pineapple (undrained)

1 21-ounce can gluten-free cherry pie filling

¾ teaspoon almond extract

¾ cup chopped walnuts

1 14-ounce can sweetened condensed milk

1 8-ounce container gluten-free nondairy whipped topping, thawed

1 With a rubber spatula, stir together the pineapple, pie filling, almond extract, walnuts, and condensed milk in a large bowl.

2 Fold in the whipped topping until completely blended.

3 Cover and chill for 3 hours. (The pudding will thicken as it sets.)

In place of the cherry pie filling and nuts, you can use gluten-free peach pie filling and coconut.

Makes 6 1-cup servings

One serving—Calories: 333; Total fat: 11.4 g; Saturated fat: 6.7 g; Cholesterol: 11 mg; Sodium: 77 mg; Carbohydrates: 49.4 g; Fiber: 1.3 g; Sugar: 46.5 g; Protein: 4.3 g

Cinnamon Baked Apples

4 medium Granny Smith apples

4 tablespoons brown sugar

1 teaspoon cinnamon

4 teaspoons butter

1. Have an adult help remove the core from each apple. Arrange the cored apples in a 9-inch round microwave-safe dish.
2. Spoon 1 tablespoon of the sugar into the cavity of each apple.
3. Place ¼ teaspoon of the cinnamon in each cavity.
4. Place 1 teaspoon of the butter on top of each apple.
5. Cover the dish with plastic wrap. Cut a small slit in the top of the plastic wrap for an air vent. Microwave on High for 3 to 4 minutes or until the apples are tender. Let stand a few minutes before serving.

You can also add raisins, nuts, gluten-free miniature marshmallows, or chopped dates to the apple cavities.

Makes 4 baked apples

One apple—Calories: 146; Total fat: 4.5 g; Saturated fat: 0 g; Cholesterol: 10 mg; Sodium: 41mg; Carbohydrates: 28.5 g; Fiber: 3.8 g; Sugar: 23.2 g; Protein: 0.3 g

Diabetic Adjustment: Use brown sugar substitute in place of the brown sugar. Use gluten-free, low-fat margarine in place of the butter.

One apple—Calories: 107; Total fat: 3.5 g; Saturated fat: 0.8 g; Cholesterol: 0 mg; Sodium: 48 mg; Carbohydrates: 21 g; Fiber: 3.7 g; Sugar: 16 g; Protein: 0.3 g

Milk-Free Adjustment: Use gluten-free, milk-free margarine in place of the butter.

Peanut Butter Baked Apples

2 apples, any variety

4 tablespoons creamy gluten-free peanut butter

2 teaspoons mini semisweet chocolate chips

24 gluten-free miniature marshmallows

1 Preheat oven to 350°F.

2 Have an adult help core the apples and slice them in half lengthwise. Spread one side of each apple half with 1 tablespoon of the peanut butter. Place the apple halves in a baking pan.

3 Sprinkle the chocolate chips on top of the peanut butter.

4 Place 6 miniature marshmallows on top of the chocolate chips on each apple.

5 Bake the apples for about 15 minutes or until the chocolate and marshmallows have melted.

6 Have an adult remove the hot pan from the oven. Caution: apples will be very hot. Let them cool before eating them.

This recipe is also good with pears instead of apples.

Makes 4 baked apple halves

One apple half—Calories: 158; Total fat: 8.8 g; Saturated fat: 1.3 g; Cholesterol: 0 mg; Sodium: 62 mg; Carbohydrates: 17.7 g; Fiber: 2.8 g; Sugar: 12.5 g; Protein: 2.6 g

Diabetic Adjustment: Use gluten-free low-sugar peanut butter. Reduce the amount of chocolate chips to 1 teaspoon. Reduce the total number of marshmallows to 12.

One apple half—Calories: 95; Total fat: 3.1 g; Saturated fat: 0.7 g; Cholesterol: 0 mg; Sodium: 46 mg; Carbohydrates: 15.7 g; Fiber: 2.2 g; Sugar: 3.9 g; Protein: 2.5 g

Winter Fruit Bowl

1 15-ounce can fruit cocktail

1 10-ounce package frozen strawberries, thawed

1 cup frozen blueberries, thawed

1 banana

½ cup gluten-free mini marshmallows

½ cup shredded coconut

1. Pour the fruit cocktail into a strainer to drain off the juice. Put the drained fruit in a medium bowl.
2. Add the strawberries (with their juice) to the bowl.
3. Stir in the blueberries.
4. Peel the banana. Slice the banana into the fruit bowl.
5. Stir in the marshmallows and coconut.
6. Cover the bowl with plastic wrap. Refrigerate fruit 1 hour before serving.

Makes 6 1-cup servings

One serving—Calories: 137; Total fat: 5.3 g; Saturated fat: 4 g; Cholesterol: 0 mg; Sodium: 9 mg; Carbohydrates: 24 g; Fiber: 4 g; Sugar: 12.3 g; Protein: 1.3 g

Diabetic Adjustment: Use fruit cocktail packed in juice (not in heavy syrup). Use unsweetened frozen strawberries. Omit the marshmallows. Use unsweetened coconut.

One serving—Calories: 85; Total fat: 5 g; Saturated fat: 4 g; Cholesterol: 0 mg; Sodium: 7 mg; Carbohydrates: 15.8 g; Fiber: 4 g; Sugar: 5.5 g; Protein: 1.3 g

Dipping Sauce for Fruit

1 16-ounce can gluten-free prepared chocolate frosting
6 ounces raspberry jam
Fresh fruits (such as apples, pears, strawberries, bananas, kiwi)

1 Spoon the frosting into a small saucepan.

2 Have an adult help you heat the frosting over medium heat, stirring frequently until it is hot and thinned.

3 Stir in the raspberry jam. Heat, stirring constantly, until the jam dissolves.

4 Pour the sauce into a bowl.

5 Cover the bowl with plastic wrap. Put the sauce in the refrigerator to chill for 3 hours or longer.

6 Just before serving, prepare the fruit. Cut apples and pears into 8 wedges each, removing seeds and cores. Wash and drain strawberries. Peel and slice bananas and kiwi into bite-sized slices.

7 To serve, place the dipping sauce in the center of a plate and surround it with the cut fruit. Provide forks for dipping the fruit.

You can also make this sauce with vanilla frosting and cinnamon apple jelly.

Makes 14 3-tablespoon servings of sauce

One serving (sauce only)—Calories: 158; Total fat: 5 g; Saturated fat: 1.5 g; Cholesterol: 0 mg; Sodium: 95 mg; Carbohydrates: 27.4 g; Fiber: 0 g; Sugar: 25.8 g; Protein: 0 g

Apple and Pear Dip

1 8-ounce package gluten-free cream cheese, softened

1 cup semisweet chocolate chips

½ cup chopped walnuts

Apples and pears for dipping

1. Spread the cream cheese on the bottom of a 9-inch glass pie plate. Sprinkle the chocolate chips over the cheese. Sprinkle the nuts over the chocolate chips.

2. Microwave on Medium (50 percent power) for 3 to 4 minutes or until warm.

3. Have an adult help you slice and core apples and pears for dipping into the sauce.

You can add coconut or spread gluten-free creamy peanut butter on top of the cream cheese before sprinkling the chocolate chips. You can use chopped peanuts in place of the walnuts.

Makes 8 ⅓-cup servings of dip

One serving (dip only)—Calories: 285; Total fat: 22.4 g; Saturated fat: 12.4 g; Cholesterol: 35 mg; Sodium: 101 mg; Carbohydrates: 20.2 g; Fiber: 0.4 g; Sugar: 15.2 g; Protein: 3 g

Saucy Fruit

Fresh, cut-up fruit such as strawberries, raspberries, blueberries, blackberries, apples, or pears

½ cup gluten-free strawberry yogurt

1 medium banana

1 tablespoon honey

1 tablespoon orange juice

¼ teaspoon cinnamon

1. Wash and drain fruit, removing cores and seeds if necessary, and cut large pieces into half-inch chunks.
2. With adult supervision, place the yogurt, banana, honey, orange juice, and cinnamon into a blender. Cover and blend for 30 seconds. Scrape the sides, then blend again for 10 seconds.
3. Pour the sauce over fresh cut-up fruit.

Makes 4 ¼-cup servings of sauce

One serving (sauce only): Calories: 55; Total fat: 0.3 g; Saturated fat: 0 g; Cholesterol: 1 mg; Sodium: 9 mg; Carbohydrates: 23.7 g; Fiber: 0.7 g; Sugar: 5.2 g; Protein: 1.1 g

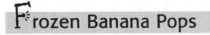rozen Banana Pops

For variety, use a different kind of cereal each time you make this.

½ cup vanilla gluten-free yogurt

1 tablespoon gluten-free peanut butter

2 teaspoons sugar

¼ teaspoon cinnamon

2 cups gluten-free cereal

¼ cup chopped peanuts

4 bananas

4 Popsicle sticks

1. Place the yogurt and peanut butter in a small bowl.
2. Add the sugar and cinnamon. Mix well.
3. Put the cereal in a quart-size, reclosable plastic bag. Use a rolling pin to crush the cereal.
4. Spread the cereal on a 12-inch square piece of waxed paper. Sprinkle the chopped peanuts on top of the cereal.
5. Peel the bananas. Insert a Popsicle stick in one end of each banana.

6 Spread the peanut butter mixture all over each banana. Lay each banana on the cereal mixture. Turn it to coat it evenly with the cereal.

7 Wrap each banana separately in plastic wrap, twisting the ends to seal it securely. Freeze the pops until ready to eat.

Makes 4 pops

One pop—Calories: 249; Total fat: 5.7 g; Saturated fat: 0.5 g; Cholesterol: 1 mg; Sodium: 148 mg; Carbohydrates: 45.7 g; Fiber: 5 g; Sugar: 15 g; Protein: 5 g

Diabetic Adjustment: Use nonfat yogurt. Use gluten-free, low-sugar peanut butter. Omit the chopped peanuts.

One pop—Calories: 214; Total fat: 2.5 g; Saturated fat: 0.3 g; Cholesterol: 1 mg; Sodium: 123 mg; Carbohydrates: 45.5 g; Fiber: 4.2 g; Sugar: 14.7 g; Protein: 3.2 g

Flower Pot Sundaes

½ pound gluten-free chocolate cookies, crushed
½ gallon gluten-free vanilla ice cream
½ cup shredded coconut
Few drops green food coloring
12 8-ounce Styrofoam cups
12 plastic flowers

1 Set aside half of the crushed cookies. Divide the remainder of the crushed cookies equally into 12 Styrofoam cups.

2 Add a scoop of ice cream to cover the cookies in each cup.

3 Sprinkle the set-aside cookie crumbs equally on top of the ice cream to look like soil.

4 Place the coconut in a sandwich-size, reclosable plastic bag. Add a few drops of green food coloring. Seal the bag, and mix well to distribute the coloring evenly. Sprinkle the coconut on top of the sundaes.

⑤ Place a plastic flower in each cup.

⑥ Freeze a minimum of 3 hours before serving.

Makes 12 sundaes

One sundae—Calories: 415; Total fat: 21.6 g; Saturated fat: 13.5 g; Cholesterol:
75 mg; Sodium: 236 mg; Carbohydrates: 50 g; Fiber: 0.6 g; Sugar: 45.8 g; Protein:
5 g

Diabetic Adjustment: Use gluten-free, sugar-free ice cream and unsweetened coconut.

One sundae—Calories: 196; Total fat: 10.4 g; Saturated fat: 5.6 g; Cholesterol: 33 mg;
Sodium: 97 mg; Carbohydrates: 24 g; Fiber: 0.3 g; Sugar: 18.3 g; Protein: 3.2 g

Fruity Pops

½ cup crushed pineapple, drained

½ cup frozen strawberries, thawed

2 cups gluten-free vanilla yogurt

1 12-ounce can frozen orange-pineapple juice concentrate, thawed

8 5-ounce paper cups

8 wooden Popsicle sticks

① Drain the can of pineapple and the strawberries in a strainer. Discard juices.

② Put the pineapple, strawberries, yogurt, and juice concentrate into a medium-size bowl. Mix them together.

③ Spoon the mixture into the paper cups. Stretch a piece of plastic wrap across the top of each cup.

④ Using a Popsicle stick, poke a hole in the plastic wrap. Stand the stick straight up in the center of the cup.

⑤ Freeze the cups for 4 or more hours.

⑥ Remove the plastic wrap, and peel away each paper cup before serving.

Makes 8 Fruity Pops

One Fruity Pop—Calories: 76; Total fat: 1 g; Saturated fat: 0 g; Cholesterol: 2 mg; Sodium: 38 mg; Carbohydrates: 20.8 g; Fiber: 0.6 g; Sugar: 17.3 g; Protein: 4 g

Diabetic Adjustment: Use pineapple packed in juice. Use unsweetened strawberries. Use fat-free, gluten-free yogurt.

One Fruity Pop—Calories: 60; Total fat: 0 g; Saturated fat: 0 g; Cholesterol: 2 mg; Sodium: 38 mg; Carbohydrates: 12.9 g; Fiber: 0.5 g; Sugar: 10.5 g: Protein: 4 g

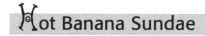

Hot Banana Sundae

1 banana

1 teaspoon honey

1 teaspoon brown sugar

¼ teaspoon cinnamon

1 scoop gluten-free vanilla ice cream

1. Preheat oven to 350°F.
2. Split the unpeeled banana lengthwise.
3. Drizzle half of the honey on each banana half.
4. Sprinkle each half with the brown sugar and cinnamon.
5. Put the halves of the banana back together. Wrap the banana in two layers of foil. Place directly on a rack in the middle of

the oven. Bake for 10 minutes. Have an adult help you remove the hot bananas from the oven.

6 Put the ice cream into a small bowl. Carefully scoop out the baked banana, and spoon it over the ice cream. (The banana will be hot, so be careful not to burn yourself.)

Makes 1 sundae

One sundae—Calories: 291; Total fat: 8 g; Saturated fat: 5 g; Cholesterol: 30 mg; Sodium: 81 mg; Carbohydrates: 64 g; Fiber: 3 g; Sugar: 24 g; Protein: 3 g

Diabetic Adjustment: Omit the honey. Use brown sugar substitute in place of the brown sugar. Use sugar-free, gluten-free ice cream.

One sundae—Calories: 177; Total fat: 4 g; Saturated fat: 2 g; Cholesterol: 13 mg; Sodium: 25 mg; Carbohydrates: 35 g; Fiber: 3 g; Sugar: 6 g; Protein: 2 g

Purple Pops

2 envelopes unflavored gluten-free gelatin

¼ cup cold water

¾ cup boiling water

1 6-ounce can frozen grape juice concentrate (not thawed)

6 3-ounce paper cups

6 Popsicle sticks

1 In a medium bowl, sprinkle the gelatin over the cold water. Let stand 1 minute to soften the gelatin.

2 Have an adult help you add the boiling water to the bowl. Stir until the gelatin is completely dissolved.

3 Stir in the frozen juice concentrate until completely dissolved.

4 With a soup ladle, pour the juice mixture into the paper cups. Freeze cups for 45 minutes until mixture begins to thicken, then insert a Popsicle stick into the center of each cup.

⑤ Freeze for 4 hours or until firm.

⑥ When ready to eat, peel off the paper cup.

In place of the grape juice concentrate, try using orange or apple juice concentrate.

Makes 6 pops

One pop—Calories: 49; Total fat: 0 g; Saturated fat: 0 g; Cholesterol: 0 mg; Sodium: 23 mg; Carbohydrates: 11 g; Fiber: 0 g; Sugar: 8 g; Protein: 0.6 g

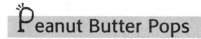Peanut Butter Pops

1 envelope unflavored gluten-free gelatin

1 cup boiling water

1 cup gluten-free peanut butter

1 cup milk

2 tablespoons gluten-free chocolate syrup

8 5-ounce paper cups

8 Popsicle sticks

① In a medium bowl, mix the gelatin with the boiling water under adult supervision. Stir until the gelatin is completely dissolved.

② With a whisk, blend in the peanut butter.

③ Stir in the milk and chocolate syrup.

④ Pour the mixture into the paper cups. Freeze cups for 45 minutes until mixture begins to thicken, then insert a Popsicle stick into the center of each cup.

⑤ Freeze pops for 4 hours or until firm.

Makes 8 Peanut Butter Pops

One Peanut Butter Pop—Calories: 223; Total fat: 17 g; Saturated fat: 2.6 g; Cholesterol: 4 mg; Sodium: 152 mg; Carbohydrates: 9.6 g; Fiber: 2 g; Sugar: 6 g; Protein: 10.2 g

Milk-Free Adjustment: Use soy milk in place of the milk.

Ice-Cream Sandwich

This recipe is fun to make because you get to choose from a variety of cookies, ice-cream flavors, and decorations.

> 2 gluten-free cookies
> 1 scoop (¼ cup) gluten-free ice cream (your favorite flavor) or
>   sherbet
> Chopped nuts, gluten-free chocolate or multicolored sprinkles,
>   coconut, or mini chocolate chips

1. Put 1 cookie on a dish, top down.
2. Put a scoop of ice cream on top of the cookie.
3. Place the remaining cookie on top of the ice cream or sherbet, top up. Roll the edges in the nuts, sprinkles, coconut, and/or chocolate chips.
4. Wrap the ice-cream sandwich in foil. Freeze for 4 hours or until firm.

Sandwich Suggestions

> Gluten-free chocolate chip cookies with gluten-free vanilla ice cream rolled in mini chocolate chips
> Gluten-free peanut butter cookies with gluten-free chocolate ice cream rolled in chopped peanuts
> Gluten-free chocolate cookies with gluten-free fudge swirl ice cream rolled in chopped walnuts
> Gluten-free lemon cookies with gluten-free lemon sherbet rolled in coconut
> Gluten-free orange cookies with gluten-free orange sherbet rolled in gluten-free multicolored sprinkles

Makes 1 ice-cream sandwich

One ice-cream sandwich (chocolate chip cookies, vanilla ice cream, and 1 tablespoon mini chocolate chips)—Calories: 227; Total fat: 9.4 g; Saturated fat: 6.1 g; Cholesterol: 15 mg; Sodium: 111 mg; Carbohydrates: 29.3 g; Fiber: 1.3 g; Sugar: 21.3 g; Protein: 2.7 g

Diabetic Adjustment: Use gluten-free, sugar-free ice cream. Use unsweetened coconut.

One ice-cream sandwich (chocolate chip cookies and vanilla ice cream)—Calories: 175; Total fat: 9.3 g; Saturated fat: 4.1 g; Cholesterol: 6 mg; Sodium: 100 mg; Carbohydrates: 20.8 g; Fiber: 1.1 g; Sugar: 9.5 g; Protein: 3.2 g

Homemade Ice Cream

1 cup milk

1 cup whipping cream

1 cup fresh raspberries,
    mashed slightly with a fork

½ cup sugar

½ teaspoon vanilla

Crushed ice

¾ cup rock salt

1 Put the milk, whipping cream, raspberries, sugar, and vanilla into a 1-pound coffee can that has a tight-fitting lid. Fasten the lid on securely.

2 Place the sealed can inside a larger 3-pound coffee can that also has a tight-fitting lid.

3 Fill the gap between the smaller can and the larger can with crushed ice.

4 Pour rock salt evenly over the ice.

5 Securely fasten the lid on the larger can.

6 Roll the sealed can back and forth on the table, floor, or sidewalk for 10 minutes or until the ice cream is thick.

Instead of the raspberries, you can add mini chocolate chips, gluten-free peanut butter, or a mashed banana.

Makes 6 ½-cup servings

One serving—Calories: 195; Total fat: 12.1 g; Saturated fat: 8.8 g; Cholesterol: 46 mg; Sodium: 34 mg; Carbohydrates: 14.3 g; Fiber: 1.3 g; Sugar: 11.6 g; Protein: 1.5 g

Personalized Parfaits

1 pint gluten-free vanilla ice cream

1 pint gluten-free chocolate ice cream

Frozen gluten-free nondairy whipped topping, thawed

Semisweet chocolate chips

Gluten-free mini marshmallows

Gluten-free chocolate syrup

Chopped nuts

Pineapple preserves

Gluten-free maraschino cherries

Gluten-free strawberry pie filling

Gluten-free multicolored sprinkles

1. Using an ice-cream scoop, scoop the ice creams into balls and place on a cookie sheet. (Work quickly so the ice cream doesn't start to melt.) Freeze the ice-cream balls until ready to serve.

2. Set out nine small bowls. Spoon a different topping into each of the bowls.

3. When ready to serve, transfer the ice-cream balls to a medium bowl.

4. Give everyone a parfait glass or dessert bowl. Place the bowls of toppings in the center of the table, and let everyone make a parfait.

Makes 8 parfaits

One parfait (1 scoop vanilla ice cream, 2 tablespoons strawberry pie filling, 2 tablespoons whipped topping, and 2 tablespoons multicolored sprinkles)— Calories: 204; Total fat: 5.5 g; Saturated fat: 3.9 g; Cholesterol: 16 mg; Sodium: 38 mg; Carbohydrates: 64.2 g; Fiber: 0.7 g; Sugar: 7.3 g; Protein: 1.3 g

Diabetic Adjustment: Use gluten-free, sugar-free ice cream.

One parfait (1 scoop vanilla ice cream, 2 tablespoons all-fruit strawberry preserves, 2 tablespoons whipped topping, and 2 tablespoons toasted unsweetened coconut)— Calories: 186; Total fat: 3.6 g; Saturated fat: 2.7 g; Cholesterol: 6 mg; Sodium: 42 mg; Carbohydrates: 36 mg; Fiber: 0.4 g; Sugar: 3.8 g; Protein 1.6 g

Crunchy Ice-Cream Sandwiches

3 cups gluten-free puffed-rice cereal

½ cup mini semisweet chocolate chips

1½ cups gluten-free peanut butter

1 pint gluten-free vanilla ice cream (or your favorite flavor),
   slightly softened

1 In a large bowl, mix the cereal, chocolate chips, and peanut butter until well blended. Spread half of the mixture in an 8-inch square pan.

2 Spread the ice cream over the cereal layer.

3 Spread the remaining cereal mixture on top of the ice cream, smoothing out the top.

4 Cover the pan with foil. Freeze for 3 hours. Cut into 3-inch squares to serve.

In place of the chocolate chips, you can add gluten-free multi-colored sprinkles or shredded coconut to the cereal mixture. Use your imagination!

Makes 9 ice-cream sandwiches

One ice-cream sandwich—Calories: 352; Total fat: 24.4 g; Saturated fat: 5.8 g; Cholesterol: 13 mg; Sodium: 169 mg; Carbohydrates: 25.1 g; Fiber: 2.2 g; Sugar: 16 g; Protein: 11.2 g

Diabetic Adjustment: Omit the chocolate chips. Use gluten-free, low-fat peanut butter. Use gluten-free, sugar-free ice cream.

One ice-cream sandwich—Calories: 318; Total fat: 16 g; Saturated fat: 3 g; Cholesterol: 23 mg; Sodium: 187 mg; Carbohydrates: 24.5 g; Fiber: 2 g; Sugar: 13.3 g; Protein: 10.2 g

Frozen Banana Sticks

1 cup shredded coconut

4 small bananas

4 Popsicle sticks

4 tablespoons gluten-free
    chocolate syrup

1. With your fingers, sprinkle coconut onto a large plate.
2. Peel the bananas. Cut a thin slice off one end of each banana.
3. Gently press a Popsicle stick into the flat end of each banana, leaving about half of the stick sticking out.
4. Pour the chocolate syrup into a small bowl.
5. Holding a banana by the stick, brush the syrup all over the banana. Immediately roll the banana in the coconut until it is evenly coated.
6. Lay the banana on a dish. Repeat the process with the other 3 bananas.
7. Cover the dish with plastic wrap, then with heavy-duty foil. Freeze at least 15 minutes.
8. Thaw slightly before eating.

In place of the chocolate syrup, you can use maple syrup. Use toasted unsweetened coconut to make this variation.

Makes 4 banana sticks

One banana stick—Calories: 241; Total fat: 7.7 g; Saturated fat: 6 g; Cholesterol: 0 mg; Sodium: 17 mg; Carbohydrates: 43.5 g; Fiber: 4.7 g; Sugar: 22 g; Protein: 1.7 g

Diabetic Adjustment: Use toasted unsweetened coconut.

One banana stick—Calories: 208; Total fat: 4.5 g; Saturated fat: 3 g; Cholesterol: 0 mg; Sodium: 6 mg; Carbohydrates: 42.7 g; Fiber: 4.7 g; Sugar: 13.2 g; Protein: 1.7 g

Raspberry Whip

1 3-ounce package gluten-free raspberry gelatin

1 cup boiling water

1 16-ounce package frozen raspberries (undrained)

1 8-ounce container gluten-free nondairy whipped topping, thawed

1. Empty the gelatin into a large bowl.
2. Have an adult help you pour the boiling water over the gelatin.
3. Stir the gelatin until it is completely dissolved.
4. Stir in the frozen raspberries until they have thawed.
5. Refrigerate the mixture for 30 minutes.
6. Remove the bowl from the refrigerator. With a whisk, whip in the whipped topping until completely blended.
7. Return the gelatin to the refrigerator for 4 hours to set, or spoon the gelatin into a 9-inch square pan, then refrigerate.

Makes 6 ¾-cup servings

One serving—Calories: 177; Total fat: 6.4 g; Saturated fat: 6.4 g; Cholesterol: 0 mg; Sodium: 33 mg; Carbohydrates: 25.6 g; Fiber: 2.8 g; Sugar: 14.2 g; Protein: 1.6 g

Diabetic Adjustment: Use gluten-free, fat-free gelatin.

One serving—Calories: 129; Total fat: 6.4 g; Saturated fat: 6.4 g; Cholesterol: 0 mg; Sodium: 37 mg; Carbohydrates: 13 g; Fiber: 2.8 g; Sugar: 4.1 g; Protein: 1 g

Peanut Butter Logs

¾ cup honey

1½ cups nonfat dry milk

1 cup gluten-free crunchy peanut butter

¼ cup mini semisweet chocolate chips

1 cup shredded coconut

1 In a bowl, stir together the honey, dry milk, peanut butter, and chocolate chips. Cover the bowl with plastic wrap. Refrigerate for 30 minutes or until the mixture holds its shape.

2 Shape the dough into two logs.

3 With your fingers, sprinkle the coconut onto a dish. Wet your hands, then use wet hands to roll the logs in the coconut.

4 Roll the coated logs in plastic wrap. Refrigerate for several hours until firm. To serve, cut the rolls into ½-inch slices.

In place of the coconut, you can use crushed nuts, crushed gluten-free cereal, or gluten-free chocolate sprinkles.

Makes 12 2-slice servings

One serving—Calories: 245; Total fat: 11.8 g; Saturated fat: 6.6 g; Cholesterol: 16 mg; Sodium: 82 mg; Carbohydrates: 31.3 g; Fiber: 0.9 g; Sugar: 21 g; Protein: 6 g

Diabetic Adjustment: Use gluten-free, low-sugar peanut butter. Omit the chocolate chips. Use toasted unsweetened coconut.

One serving—Calories: 190; Total fat: 8.5 g; Saturated fat: 4.1 g; Cholesterol: 16 mg; Sodium: 77 mg; Carbohydrates: 24.9 g; Fiber: 0.9 g; Sugar: 16.3 g; Protein: 5.9 g

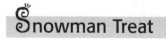Snowman Treat

4 tablespoons (½ stick) gluten-free margarine

1 10-ounce package gluten-free marshmallows

¼ teaspoon vanilla

6 cups gluten-free puffed-rice cereal

Gluten-free decorator icing

1 Have an adult help you melt the margarine in a large saucepan over low heat.

2 When the margarine has melted, add the marshmallows and vanilla. Stir until the marshmallows have melted completely.

3 Remove the pan from the stove. Stir in the cereal until the puffed rice is completely coated.

4 Spray a small bowl and a medium-sized bowl with gluten-free nonstick spray. Spread the cereal mixture in the bowls.

5 Spray the back of a spoon with gluten-free nonstick spray. Use the back of the spoon to carefully press down on the cereal mixture so the tops are level.

6 Set the bowls in the refrigerator for 30 minutes to set.

7 Unmold the bowls onto a large dish, with the smaller mound of cereal mixture on top of the larger one.

8 Use the tube of decorator icing to complete your snowman by drawing eyes, nose, mouth, buttons, and a scarf around the neck. Break off pieces of snowman to serve.

For Halloween, use this recipe to make a jack-o'-lantern treat. Before adding the cereal to the margarine mix, stir in ½ teaspoon of yellow food coloring and ⅛ teaspoon of red food coloring. (The color combination will make orange.) Pat the cereal mixture into one large bowl. After it sets in the refrigerator for 30 minutes, invert it onto a plate, and you will have a pumpkin! All it needs is gluten-free black decorator icing to make the eyes and mouth.

Makes 12 ½-cup servings

One serving—Calories: 99; Total fat: 4.8 g; Saturated fat: 1.4 g; Cholesterol: 4 mg; Sodium: 50 mg; Carbohydrates: 16 g; Fiber: 0 g; Sugar: 10 g; Protein: 0.6 g

Cookie and Cake Decorations

¾ cup gluten-free marshmallow creme

1½ cups confectioners' sugar

Gluten-free decorating gel in a variety of colors

1 In a medium bowl, mix the marshmallow creme and 1 cup of the sugar.

2 Knead the mixture.

3 Turn the mixture out onto a cutting board.

④ With your hands, work in the remaining ½ cup of sugar until it is completely blended.

⑤ Work in the food coloring, or divide the dough into several pieces and color each piece a different color.

⑥ Form the dough into desired shapes. Use the shapes to decorate the top of a frosted cake or cookie.

Makes 32 1-tablespoon servings

One serving—Calories: 10; Total fat: 0.4 g; Saturated fat: 0 g; Cholesterol: 0 mg; Sodium: 1 mg; Carbohydrates: 2.4 g; Fiber: 0 g; Sugar: 2.1 g; Protein: 0 g

8

Kitchen Projects

Pomander Ball

Place the pomander on the kitchen counter to make the kitchen smell good. Or make several pomanders, and arrange them in a bowl for a sweet-smelling centerpiece.

    1 small orange
    Thin ribbon
    ½ teaspoon cinnamon
    100 whole cloves

 Tie the ribbon around the orange, making a bow at the top.

Put some cinnamon in a sandwich-size, reclosable plastic bag. Add the cloves. Seal the bag, and shake it to coat the cloves with spice.

Push the cloves into the orange. Continue inserting cloves until the entire surface of the orange is covered (except where the ribbon is).

Edible Play Dough

This play dough may be kept in an airtight plastic container for up to 3 days.

> 1 cup gluten-free peanut butter
> ¾ cup light corn syrup
> ¼ cup honey
> 1¼ cups confectioners' sugar
> 1¼ cups nonfat dry milk

1. Put the peanut butter, corn syrup, honey, confectioners' sugar, and milk in a medium bowl.
2. With your hands, mix the ingredients thoroughly. Do not refrigerate the dough.

Kitchen Garden

As the days pass, you will see your vegetable or pineapple grow roots. Organic vegetables and fruits sprout sooner and healthier because they are not treated with growth retardants and inhibitors.

> 1 widemouthed glass jar or plastic bowl
> 1 organic potato, sweet potato, yam, or pineapple top
> 4 to 6 toothpicks

1. Fill the jar or bowl with water.
2. Push toothpicks into the vegetable or fruit so that the toothpicks balance on the outside rim of the container and the bottom part of the fruit is partially immersed in the water.
3. Set the container on the kitchen counter for several weeks. Add water every few days to keep the bottom part of the vegetable or fruit in water.

Bubbles

You can create these fun bubbles using a slotted spoon if you don't have an empty spool.

> 2 cups warm water
>
> 2 tablespoons liquid dish detergent
>
> 1 tablespoon sugar
>
> 1 empty thread spool

1. In a bowl, stir together the water, detergent, and sugar.
2. Dip one end of the spool into the soap mixture. Blow bubbles through the spool from the dry end.

Tree Ornaments

The variety of ornaments you can make is unlimited.

> 2 cups Gluten-Free Flour Mixture (See the Hints chapter.)
>
> 1 cup salt
>
> ¾ to 1 cup water
>
> Paints (water, acrylic, or oil-based)
>
> Clear varnish

1. Preheat oven to 325°F.
2. Stir the flour mixture and salt together in a medium bowl.
3. Add ¾ cup of water and stir. If the mixture is too dry, add another ¼ cup of water.
4. Knead the dough for 10 minutes.
5. With a rolling pin, roll out the dough on a cutting board to ¼ inch thick.
6. Use cookie cutters to cut out shapes.
7. Use a straw to make a hole near the top of each shape for hanging the ornament.

8. Line a cookie sheet with foil.
9. Place the ornaments on top of the foil.
10. Bake for 35 to 40 minutes or until the ornaments are hard.
11. Have an adult help you remove the hot tray from the oven. Let the ornaments cool.
12. Paint the ornaments and let them dry. Apply a coat of varnish to all sides to preserve the ornaments.
13. Tie a string through the hole of each ornament.

Scented Gift Ornaments

When you give these ornaments as gifts, attach a note to each one saying that it is to be hung in a closet to give off a wonderful scent. These ornaments are also nice to hang from the rearview mirror of a car to give it a pleasing aroma.

1 cup cinnamon
1 tablespoon ground cloves
1 tablespoon nutmeg
¾ cup applesauce
2 tablespoons white glue
Ribbon

1. In a medium bowl, stir together the cinnamon, cloves, and nutmeg.
2. Stir in the applesauce and glue.
3. With your hands, knead the dough for 3 minutes or until the dough is smooth and all the ingredients are well blended.
4. Working with small batches of dough, roll out each batch to ¼-inch thickness.
5. Use cookie cutters to cut the dough into desired shapes.
6. Use a toothpick to make a small hole near the top of each ornament.

7. Place the ornaments on a wire rack. Allow them to dry for several days at room temperature. Turn the ornaments over each day so they dry evenly.

8. Thread a piece of ribbon through each hole for hanging.

Face Paint

Painting faces is fun, whether you are the clown for a backyard circus, dressing up for Halloween, or just playing with friends.

2 teaspoons solid vegetable shortening

5 teaspoons cornstarch

1 teaspoon Gluten-Free Flour Mixture (See the Hints chapter.)

Glycerin (available at pharmacies)

Food coloring (optional)

1. Put the shortening, cornstarch, and flour mixture on a large dinner plate. Stir with a small spoon to form a smooth paste. Add 3 or 4 drops of glycerin for a creamy texture.

2. The mixture you now have will be a wonderful white that you may apply. But if you wish to color your paint, divide the mixture into several different small piles on your dish. Stir 2 drops of food coloring into each pile.

Eggseptional Garden

The eggs in this garden can have either straight (using grass) or curly (using parsley) hair.

1 egg
Felt-tipped markers
1 empty egg carton
Potting soil
Grass seed
Water mister

1. Carefully crack the egg in half over a bowl, letting the egg whites and yolks drop into the bowl. (Cover the bowl with plastic wrap and refrigerate the insides of the eggs to be used in a different recipe.) Rinse out both halves of the shells, then dry them *very* carefully, so you don't break the shells.

2. With the rounded side of each half shell facing down, use markers to paint a funny face on each half shell. (Don't press hard, or the shell will break.)

3. Place the egg halves in the egg carton or in an egg holder.

4. Gently fill each half with potting soil. Sprinkle grass seed on top of the soil. Water the seed with a water mister, or very lightly sprinkle with water.

5. Place near a sunny window, and watch your garden grow.

6. When the faces you drew on your eggs look like they have a full head of hair, plant the eggs in your garden outside, shell and all.

Sugar Igloo

5-inch cardboard circle
100 sugar cubes
3 egg whites
2½ cups confectioners' sugar

1. Lay a base row of sugar cubes around the edge of the cardboard, leaving a space for the igloo entrance.
2. Make a glue by mixing the egg whites with enough confectioners' sugar in a small bowl to form a paste. Add a few drops of water if the glue gets too thick to work with.
3. Spread a little bit of paste on the bottom of a sugar cube, and set the cube on top of the first row of sugar cubes. Continue with more sugar cubes, staggering the cubes so they do not line up exactly with the ones on the layer below. Complete a second row, keeping the entrance of the igloo open.
4. Continue building rows with the paste and sugar cubes. With each row, set the cubes a little closer to the center of the circle so that you gradually lessen the circumference of (distance around) the igloo.
5. After 5 layers, let the cubes dry for several hours before adding more layers. There should be a total of 10 layers.
6. Make the doorway arch separately by laying the sugar cubes in the shape of an arch and pasting them together. When the arch is dry, paste it in place on the igloo.
7. Allow the completed igloo to dry overnight.

Vinegar Painting

Different colored paper can be used for different seasons: for fall, cut brown tissue paper into leaf shapes. For spring, cut orange and green tissue paper into flowers and leaves.

Red tissue paper
¼ cup white vinegar
1 thin paintbrush
White construction paper

1. Cut small heart shapes from the tissue paper.
2. Pour the vinegar into a small bowl.
3. Brush vinegar over an area of the construction paper. Lay a tissue paper heart over the brushed area. Repeat this process with the remaining hearts.
4. As the vinegar dries, the tissue paper will fall off, leaving red heart prints on the construction paper.

Building Blocks

You can create colorful blocks by mixing the marshmallows with boxes of various gluten-free gelatins in large, reclosable plastic bags.

Gluten-free marshmallows (large and/or small)
Toothpicks with rounded edges

1. Insert toothpicks into the marshmallows to create your own building blocks.
2. Connect the marshmallows to construct different types of buildings, such as castles, igloos, or forts.

Bean Sprouts

Bean sprouts are edible. Try adding them to salads.

1 paper towel
1 reclosable, sandwich-size plastic bag
Water
4 dried beans

1. Place the paper towel inside the plastic bag.
2. Add just enough water to dampen the paper towel.

3 Add the beans to the bag. Seal the bag and store it in a dark place for four days, adding a few drops of water to the bag if the paper towel is dry.

4 Once the sprouts appear, place the bag on a windowsill where it can get sunlight.

5 When the sprouts are ½-inch long, transfer them to a shallow dish. Sprinkle them lightly with water each day. In about a week, the sprouts should be ready for harvesting.

Bird Feeder

Hang this bird feeder close to the house in the winter so you can watch the birds feed.

1 slice bread (gluten-free, of course)
1 toothpick
String
2 tablespoons gluten-free peanut butter
3 tablespoons birdseed

1 Using a cookie cutter, cut out a shape from the center of the bread.

2 Let the bread shape dry for two days in the open air.

3 With a toothpick, poke a hole near the top of the bread shape.

4 Thread a piece of string through the hole.

5 Spread both sides of the bread with peanut butter.

6 Sprinkle both sides with birdseed.

7 Hang the bird feeder from a tree or a fence, tying the strings around a branch or fence post.

Milk Painting

This is an edible project in which bread can be decorated for holidays and special occasions using Easter egg, pumpkin, or heart designs.

>   2 tablespoons milk
>   2 3-ounce paper cups
>   1 drop each of 2 different food colorings
>   1 new, thin paintbrush
>   1 slice bread (gluten-free, of course)

1 Pour 1 tablespoon of milk into each of the paper cups.
2 Put 1 drop of food coloring into one cup and 1 drop of the other food coloring into the other cup.
3 Using a new, thin paintbrush, paint the bread with a design or your name. (Don't use so much milk paint that your bread becomes soggy.)
4 Toast your bread, and see the finished creation!

Eggshell Art

Spring is a great time to make this project using colorful eggshells from Easter.

>   Eggshells
>   Felt-tipped markers or crayons
>   1 piece of paper
>   Glue

 Whenever you or someone else uses an egg for cooking, save the shell. Rinse them well, then lay them on paper towels till they are completely dried. Store them in a reclosable plastic bag.
2 Break the dried eggshells into tiny bits.

③ With markers or crayons, draw simple pictures on a piece of paper (for example, a kite, flower, fish, teddy bear, or airplane).

④ Spread glue inside the outlined picture.

⑤ Sprinkle the bits of broken eggshells onto the glue. Allow this to dry for 2 hours. You may paint the eggshells after the glue has dried.

Gumdrop Christmas Tree

Vary the size of the trees you create by using large gluten-free gumdrops.

> 1 box toothpicks
> 1 bag small gluten-free gumdrops
> 1 10-inch Styrofoam cone

① Push a toothpick into the bottom of a gumdrop. Push the other end into the side of the cone, starting near the bottom. (If you start at the top, the cone will get top-heavy and fall over.)

② Continue attaching gumdrops, working your way up the cone, until the cone is covered in gumdrops.

Candy Wreath

Make a candy wreath for every season: use root beer and butterscotch candies with yellow and black ribbon for Halloween. Pink and yellow ribbons can be paired with individually wrapped, gluten-free, pastel jelly candies for spring.

> 1 sturdy wire coat hanger
> Masking tape
> Curling ribbon
> 2 pounds assorted wrapped gluten-free hard candies

1. Have an adult help you unbend the coat hanger and shape it into an 8-inch circle. Twist the wire around the top, leaving the hook intact.

2. Wrap the entire circle with masking tape. (This keeps the curling ribbon from slipping.)

3. With a 2-inch piece of curling ribbon, tie one end of a candy to the wreath. Continue doing this, tying candies in different directions so they form a semicircle around the wire, until the circle is tightly covered with candies.

4. Wrap ribbon around the top of the hanger. Tie a bow at the bottom of the hook.

arshmallow Snowman

You can create a family of snowmen by using miniature marshmallows to make the children.

3 large gluten-free marshmallows
5 toothpicks
Orange felt-tipped marker
Gluten-free decorating gel
1 gluten-free chocolate kiss

1. Push a toothpick halfway into the center of a marshmallow. Place a second marshmallow on top of the first, pushing the other half of the toothpick through it to hold it in place. Push a second toothpick halfway through the top of the second marshmallow. Place the third marshmallow on top of the second, pushing the other half of the toothpick through to hold it in place.

2. Use broken pieces of toothpicks for the arms. With a marker, color a broken piece of toothpick orange. Insert it into the top marshmallow for the nose. Use decorating gel to make the eyes, mouth, and buttons.

③ Put a little glob of decorating gel on the top of the top marshmallow, then place the candy kiss on the gel for a hat. (Once the gel sets, it will act as glue and hold the "hat" on.)

Homemade Barrettes

This craft uses a glue gun, so it requires adult supervision. If the candies are coated with polyurethane, the barrettes should last for years.

> Small holiday candy (for example, candy corn for fall, jelly beans for Easter)
> 1 metal barrette (available at craft stores)
> Sponge-type "paintbrush"
> Clear polyurethane
> String

① Using a glue gun, hot-glue candies onto the barrette.
② With the sponge brush, cover the candies completely with polyurethane. Thread a piece of string through the barrette and hang it from the bottom of a hanger. Hang the hanger in a well-ventilated open space. Let the barrette dry 24 hours.
③ Apply a second coat of polyurethane. Let it dry 24 hours.

Potpourri

For variety, you may add miniature pinecones, bay leaves, and dried leaves and petals from other flowers to your potpourri.

> 3 cups fresh rose petals
> 1 tablespoon ground cloves
> 1 tablespoon nutmeg
> 1 tablespoon cinnamon
> 2 tablespoons brown sugar

1 Spread rose petals in a single layer on paper towels. Let dry 1 week.

2 In a bowl, gently mix the dried petals and the cloves, nutmeg, cinnamon, and brown sugar.

3 To scent a room, place the mixture in a bowl. To scent a drawer, place in a small fabric bag, or lay it on several layers of tulle netting, then bring the sides together and tie with a ribbon.

Pictures from the Kitchen

Supplies from the kitchen are perfect to use for maps for school projects or for scenic collages. Draw your picture first with crayons, then enhance the picture by gluing kitchen supplies on top. Use any of the following items for your project, or let your imagination run wild:

A cinnamon stick for a tree trunk and bay leaves for the leaves of the tree

Toothpicks for fences

Sesame seeds for a gravel driveway

Small elbow macaroni (gluten-free, of course) for a tile roof

Red candy hearts for flowers

Chocolate sprinkles, fresh coffee grounds, or cocoa for dirt

Foil for a frozen pond or ice-skating

Blue plastic wrap for pool water

Confectioners' sugar or cotton balls for clouds

Eggshells for house siding

Cut-up napkins for curtains

Index